WORKING DRESS IN COLONIAL AND REVOLUTIONARY AMERICA

WORKING DRESS IN COLONIAL AND REVOLUTIONARY AMERICA

Peter F. Copeland

Contributions in American History, Number 58

Greenwood Press
Westport, Connecticut • London, England

Library of Congress Cataloging in Publication Data

Copeland, Peter F.
    Working dress in colonial and Revolutionary America.

    (Contributions in American history; no. 58)
    Bibliography: p.
    Includes index.
    1. Costume—United States. 2. Costume—History—18th
century. I. Title.
GT607.C66   391'.04'33170973   76-15309
ISBN 0-8371-9033-9

The illustrations from Peter Copeland, *Everyday Dress of the
American Revolution*, Dover Publications, New York, 1975,
are used with the permission of Dover Publications.

Library of Congress Catalog Card Number: 76-15309
ISBN 0-8371-9033-9

First published in 1977

Greenwood Press, Inc.
51 Riverside Avenue, Westport, Connecticut 06880

Printed in the United States of America

To Donna Casey, without whose patient and
astute assistance, discerning advice, and affection
this book would never have been completed.

Contents

Acknowledgments

The author would like to thank the following persons for the time and interest they have taken in this book, and the advice and assistance they have given in gathering the material that went into the writing and illustrations: Albert Haarman, Donald W. Holst, Dr. Melvin H. Jackson, Robert L. Klinger, Dr. Harold D. Langley, Diana McGeorge, Fitzhugh McMaster, and Marko Zlatich.

In researching and preparing the illustrations, the author relied upon a variety of contemporary documents and published accounts. A number of illustrations were taken directly from such sources, and, in these instances, the original illustrator is credited. All illustrations noted as "by the author" were drawn for this volume by Peter F. Copeland.

Introduction

From portraits painted by the leading artists of the day, as well as newspapers, monthly journals, travel accounts, letters, diaries, and account books, we have a fairly complete picture of how the American upper class dressed in the eighteenth century. As a result of these available sources, several important illustrated works on the colonial dress of the more affluent have been published.[1] But what reliable picture do we have of the working class of the period? Unfortunately, eighteenth-century America did not produce a William Hogarth, a Marcellus Laroon, or a William Henry Pyne, as England did, to depict the common people of the city streets or the rural farm folk of that era. Nor does the literature furnish an abundance of material on the occupational dress of the working class. By the time the artists of the new nation turned their talents to graphic portrayals of the soldiers, laborers, and pioneers of the period, a generation or more had gone by, and their portraits were largely romanticized and inaccurate. Hence, the common people of colonial America who lived through the years of the American Revolution passed from the view of history undepicted in their own time. It is difficult for the historical researcher of today to determine with any real accuracy the actual appearance and dress of, say, a fishmonger of Boston, a street peddler of New York, or a frontier militia man of rural Virginia.

In the main, then, we must depend on inference and European sources. Insofar as the typical eighteenth-century free American worker was a West European and only a generation or two removed from his homeland, it may be safely concluded that his occupational dress was, for the most part, the same as that of the English working class. Exceptions were found in New York, Pennsylvania, and North Carolina, where, respectively, the Dutch, German, and Highland Scots influences remained and in the more simple frontier areas which adopted the Indian blanket coats, leggings, moccasins, moose skin breeches, fringed hunting shirts, fur caps, and breech clouts. Whatever differences there existed between English and colonial dress were owing to the

American worker's greater affluence. Working men in the colonies commanded higher wages than did their cousins in Europe; thus it was that the American generally wore cleaner and better clothing. A number of contemporary witnesses have attested to the American's superior appearance. The Chevalier Felix de Beaujour observed that "of all that pleases a stranger when arriving in the U.S. nothing is more pleasing than the external cleanliness noticeable everywhere in the streets, the houses, the clothing. Everybody is decently dressed. The men wear woolen suits, the women cloth dresses generally white, always with clean linen and nobody is seen in public with those hideous rags so distressing in other countries."[2]

This is not to say that poverty and oppression did not exist in eighteenth-century America. As in Europe, beggars, street singers, pickpockets, runaway servants, and unemployed seamen wandered the streets; thieves, prostitutes, and swindlers lived in the underworld of the cities; and robbers and highwaymen preyed upon travelers and coaches in rural areas. And, too, poor farmers scratched out a bare existence from the land as did their counterparts across the Atlantic. In America, however, the problems of poverty and crime were never as widespread as in Europe.

The more flexible class system that developed in American contributed to the colonist's relatively higher standard of living. At the beginning of the century, however, this flexibility had not been the case. As in England, the classes were then more rigidly stratified, with the planter aristocrats of Virginia, Maryland, and South Carolina, the patroon landowners of New York, and the wealthy merchants of New England forming a small, but influential, upper class. As the century progressed and land became more easily acquired, with a little effort and luck many a working man was able to increase his modest holdings and become a well-to-do member of the middle class. Others became independent craftsmen, shopkeepers, and tavern owners. Those who were not so fortunate remained locked into the lower class; these were the tenant farmers, unskilled laborers, seafarers, and hired men, and, at the very bottom of the class, the indentured servants, redemptioners, indigent poor, and the black slaves. It is with the dress of these—the middle and lower classes—that this book will be concerned.

Working class dress differed considerably from the fashionable attire of the upper classes, both in material and cut. The worker's garments were simpler, looser, and more functional in design. They were made of coarser woven fabrics (often homespun) and were devoid of embroidered buttonholes, ruffles, tinsel lace, and other embellishments so cherished by the wealthy. In color, working class garments were generally drab whereas the upper classes favored brilliant scarlets and yellows. Whereas fine, brilliant white Holland linen was worn by the wealthy, unbleached, coarse linen of a pale yellowish brown was the material used in making the shirts, smocks, and aprons of the working class.

The items of clothing worn by the two classes also differed. Gentlemen wore fashionable knee breeches, eschewing the trousers popular with the working man which they considered rude garments symbolic of the lower orders of society. The working man, on the other hand, found trousers more practical and comfortable than the tight knee breeches for performing his laboring tasks. Those who did own knee breeches would have them made of leather or some other stout and durable material. In addition, workmen preferred jackets to the stylish long coats. The lower class headgear consisted of uncocked hats with the brim of the hat down all around. In contrast, the gentlemen almost invariably wore their hats cocked up, except for hunting and other sports activities. Wigs were worn by all classes. As one foreign visitor remarked in the 1740s: "All men wore them, clod-hoppers, day laborers, in a word, all laboring folk go through their daily duties all with perukes on their heads."[3] Farmers wore wigs even while plowing.

A formal suit of clothing was a scarce commodity for the working man. For those who did own one, if well made it would be expected to last for two or more generations. Hence, it was treasured and saved for special occasions such as Sunday church services, marriages, and funerals. Since good cloth and fine linen were acquired only with the greatest difficulty, other articles of clothing were also carefully preserved: gowns, ruffled linen body shirts, laced and bound beaver hats, or shoes with silver buckles were all precious commodities.

The cut and color of garments were certain indicators of social class. In eighteenth-century America, the man on the street could identify the occupation of a passerby simply by looking at his garments and the accoutrements he wore or carried. The cobbler was recognized by his blackened leather apron; the butcher by his blue apron, protective sleeves, sharpen-steel, and case of knives secured at his waist; the sailor by his Monmouth cap and tarred trousers; the waggoner by his long frock and bull whip. This was the case among some upper class professions as well. The doctor, for example, was known by his black suit, "physical wig," and gold-handled walking stick.

The working woman was also easily identifiable. Her gown was meaner and shorter than the lady's. She had no hoops under her skirt, and her rough linen or cheap cotton apron was coarse and functional rather than ruffled and decorated. The elaborate printed textile and embroidered cloth, which was so dear to the colonial lady's heart, was seldom seen on the working class woman. She had to content herself with the simple checks, stripes, and spotted patterns available to her class.

While ready-made clothing could be had in shops, it was a very small industry. Ready-made garments were of the meanest variety, being manufactured only for some of the lower class occupations. Sailor's garments could be purchased ready-made at waterfront "slop shops." Black slaves on plantations in the rural South were sometimes given ready-made jackets and breeches of "negro cloth" or "negro cotton" which had been made and bought in England. Soldiers were issued ready-made suits of uniform clothing when available; during the American Revolution, in fact, the Congress imported many such uniforms from France. Finally, the leather breeches of the laborer were also ready-made. As these garments were cheap, yet strong, and very difficult to make up at home, the merchants found a good market for them among the working population.[4]

The manufacture of textiles in the colonies was primarily a household industry, particularly among the poor and in rural areas. Coarse homespun linens and woolens were produced throughout the northern and middle colonies. Many families could manufacture enough homespun textiles both to clothe themselves and to sell the surplus in their neighborhood. By 1791, Dr. Alexander Hamilton estimated that three-fourths of all the clothing worn in the United States was made up from locally produced cloth.

*   *   *

This book encompasses the period 1710 through 1810. It will be noted that in the period before mass-produced, ready-made clothing became available, the styles worn by working people changed very little from one century to the other. Thus, the dress of the farmer, waggoner, or sailor, for example, did not change significantly during the hundred-year span presented here. The dress or urban workers and skilled craftsmen underwent greater change because they deliberately imitated the upper class fashions.

NOTES

1. E.g., Alice Morse Earle, *Two Centuries of Costume in America* (New York, 1903); and Edward Warwick, Henry C. Pitz, and Alexander Wyckoff, *Early American Dress: The Colonial and Revolutionary Periods* (New York, 1965).
2. Chevalier Felix de Beaujour, *Aperçu des Etats Unis* (Paris, 1814).
3. Phillis Cunnnigton, Catherine Lucas, and Alan Mansfield, *Occupational Costume in England from the Eleventh Century to 1914* (London, 1967), p. 31.
4. Claudia Kidwell and Margaret Christman, *Suiting Everyone* (Washington, D.C., 1974).

WORKING DRESS IN COLONIAL AND REVOLUTIONARY AMERICA

(1)
Seafarers and Fishermen

part 1. The Sailor

At the outbreak of the Revolution the American colonies had developed a flourishing merchant marine. Indeed, shipping had become perhaps the second largest business in colonial America, being surpassed only by agriculture, and was as developed as that of many leading European nations. A foreign visitor to America during the Revolutionary War, the Abbé Robin, observed that America's "shipyards established in all their ports have made them the rivals of the best constructors of the old world. The commerce of Boston furnished to Britain masts and yards for the Royal Navy. The Americans constructed on commission, or for their own account, a large number of merchant ships reknown for the superiority of their sailing powers."[1]

In the seacoast cities, from Maine to Georgia, maritime workers, seamen, fishermen, and boatmen made up the largest percentage of the working class. In the town of Newport, Rhode Island, for example, nearly every male over the age of sixteen went to sea at some time or other in his life.[2]

The colonial merchant crew was in the main dominated by the lower classes and social outcasts: deserters from the Army, escaped criminals, runaway indentured servants and apprentices, adventurous youths lured by the romance of the sea who were ultimately destined for a farmer's life, and seafaring migrants—"old timers" who had no other shoreside address than that of a waterfront tavern keeper. Shorthanded vessels would also take men tricked into signing on by the waterfront crimps who often ran seamen's boarding houses.

The life of these seamen was little easier than the one they had left. Conditions aboard ship were primitive and unhealthy. Most ships were infested with rats and vermin. While the merchant seaman was not as badly paid or as brutally treated as his counterpart in the Navy, he was still considered an outcast and an inferior by most citizens ashore. The sailors were in such bad repute that some seaports passed legislation forbidding them from going ashore after sundown. Another harsh law prohibited seamen from traveling

Figure 1. *Dutch Sailor from the Northern Netherlands, 1694.*
The fur cap, short jacket with flaring skirts, and petticoat
trousers are much like those worn by Western seamen throughout the eighteenth century. This type of cap and jacket, however, seems to have been more commonly worn by Dutch
sailors and fishermen than by seafarers of other nations.

Source: An engraving by J. and C. Luiken, "het Menselyk
Bedrfy," Amsterdam, 1694, courtesy of the British Museum;
C. R. Boxer, *The Dutch Seaborn Empire, 1600-1800* (London,
1965).

on shore without producing a certificate of discharge
from their last vessel. Other laws permitted any free
white person to catch runaway seamen and forbade
tavern keepers from entertaining seamen in their estab-
lishments for more than one hour a day.[3]

While the maritime industry was a thriving one,
like other industries it too was subject to economic
swings. For example, the end of the French and Indian
War and the depression that followed it left many seamen unable to find work and living in poverty in colonial
seaports. Many of the mob riots that shook the cities
of colonial America before the Revolution were fomented
by seafarers "on the beach." Indeed, Crispus Attucks
and others who participated in the Boston Massacre in
1769 were unemployed seamen. According to Jesse
Lemisch, American seamen played an important political part in the events leading to the Revolution and,
once war came, they almost unanimously took up the
rebel cause with enthusiasm.[4]

NAVY LIFE

Most Royal naval vessels of the eighteenth century
formed their crews through impressment; that is, press
gangs forcibly took men from the streets and jails of both
English and colonial towns and from merchant and
fishing vessels, regardless of nationality. In colonial
America the forays of Royal Navy press gangs were
sometimes violently resisted by mob action. Impressment caused riots in several colonial cities; an especially
violent one in Boston in 1747 led to some attempts to
restrict the practice.[5]

According to Benjamin Franklin, during the French
and Indian War impressment was more injurious to
colonial trade than the activities of the enemy. Colonial
seaports were hard hit by this practice. In one of the
more spectacular raids, eight hundred men were impressed in New York City in 1757. Manpower along
the waterfront and in the colonial fishing fleets suffered massively. The Royal Navy press gangs operated
in American ports until the beginning of the Revolu-

tion and continued thereafter in the areas under British occupation. During the Revolution, the Continental Navy also practiced impressment, though on a much more modest level than the British.[6]

Living conditions aboard a man-of-war were even worse than on a merchant vessel. Sanitary arrangements were inadequate, and ventilation below decks was poor. Disease was often rampant, especially in tropical waters, and many deaths resulted from scurvy, yellow fever, and dysentery. As a further complication, there was generally a shortage of surgeons' mates aboard.

Finally, the Navy man had to contend with flogging which sometimes brought death or crippling to the victim. Small wonder, then, that service in the Navy was regarded as none too desirable. During the American Revolution, naval service was deemed such a punishment that "incorrigible" soldiers were often drafted from the Army into the Navy.[7]

SEAMAN'S DRESS

The British seafarer's clothing did not become a truly distinctive and well-defined occupational dress until the early eighteenth century. In fact, until the sixteenth century the seaman's dress had hardly differed from that of any other worker. Once the sailor's dress became individualized, however, it seems that further significant change was not to take place for decades to come: the seaman wore much the same kind of clothing, both in material and cut, at the beginning of the eighteenth century as at the end. For example, the *Pennsylvania Gazette* notice of a runaway apprentice from the ship *Mary* at Philadelphia in January 1729 mentioned that he had on "a light colored jacket with canvas patches on the shoulders, canvas trousers, light grey stockings and a hat."[8] Such a description would easily have fit a seafarer fifty years later.

Naval crew members were not issued formal uniforms except in such special cases as the crews of captains' gigs or admirals' barges. These boat crews were often fancifully dressed at the pleasure and expense of the

Figure 2. *Sailor of the Royal Navy, Circa 1730.*
The most distinctive feature of this dress is the jacket, the upper half of which is double-breasted and the lower half single-breasted. About his neck is the sailor's neckerchief. The buttons on the jacket seem to be of metal.

Source: An unidentified print in the author's collection, entitled "Savage Mostyn, Rear Admiral." Savage Mostyn became a naval lieutenant in 1734, captain in 1739, vice admiral, commander of the North American station in 1757, in which year he died. The above portrait was probably done when he was a midshipman.

5

Figure 3. *Seaman of the Royal Navy, 1737.*
The striped waistcoat cut straight along the bottom is unusual
for this period. The trousers are cut full and have a fly front.
    Source: An etching entitled "The British Hercules,"
British Museum.

officer in command. Thus, Admiral Anson (George,
Lord Anson) in 1743, had the crew of his barge dressed
in scarlet jackets and blue silk waistcoats trimmed in
silver.

Sailors and merchant seamen were issued clothing
from the ship's "slop chest." The "slop chest" or
ship's store, established in the British Navy in 1623,
was stocked by naval "slop sellers" (contractors) in the
Royal Navy and by the ship's owner in the merchant
marine. It supplied much the same type of garments
("necessaries for the clothing of the men") for crew
members.[9]

Excepted from the issue of clothing were men who
had been impressed. Insofar as they were required to
serve only to the conclusion of whatever war was then
being waged, it was thought a waste of money to provide
them clothing. Only men brought aboard in destitute
condition would receive clothing from the purser.[10]

American sailors and merchant seamen dressed much
the same as their seafaring brothers in Europe: short,
wide trousers variously termed "slivers," "slops," or
"petticoat trousers," which were worn both on board
and ashore; jackets, waistcoats, and body shirts, which
were the usual upper garments; kerchief; a variety of
headgear, including cocked or uncocked, knitted, and
leather hats; gloves; and buckled shoes.

"Slops," or "petticoat trousers," were often made
of canvas or oznabrug linen, although they were sometimes of striped or checked material. They were principally worn at sea to protect breeches or other under-
garments from dirt, tar, paint, and rust while the men
were working on deck. Many pictures of the period
show that slops were also worn ashore. While breeches
are seldom seen in illustrations of the period, they
were worn by American seamen. In 1778, aboard the
ship *Dragon* of the Virginia State Navy, sixty suits of
clothes consisting of cloth jackets, linen shirts, and
flannel breeches were made up for the seamen.[11]
White jackets and breeches were issued to the men of
the *Hero* galley of the Virginia State Navy in 1779.

Trousers were worn in a variety of styles, the most

Figure 4. *The British Sailor's Loyal Toast, 1738.*
Two of the sailors wear small, round hats cocked up on three
sides, a style that did not become common among seamen
until 1750. Two sailors may have knitted caps under their
hats. Three have hats with white binding on the brims. Only
the sailor on the far left is wearing a vest. The sailor on the
far right has on a body shirt with a fringed lower edge, not
tucked into his trousers. All wear single-breasted seamen's
jackets and wide, full short trousers, probably petticoat
trousers, though in this case they reach well below the knees.
All wear buckled shoes.

Source: An unidentified print in the author's collection.

popular being the "long trousers" or "narrow trousers,"
which were straight and fairly close-fitting in the leg,
sometimes tapering slightly to the ankle. They were
usually fastened with two buttons at the waistband
and two buttons on a straight fly front[12] and invariably terminated at the ankle, or above, never falling
over the shoe as became the fashion in the nineteenth
century. Other trousers were full and straight but ended
halfway between knee and ankle. A few had a fall front
similar to most breeches of the period. Descriptions of
runaway seamen and naval deserters, which remain our
best evidence for eighteenth-century seaman's dress,
also mention canvas trousers, ticklenburg trousers
(linen trousers), trousers of blue and brown cloth, and
"bays" trousers (for tropical wear in the Royal Navy).
Samuel Kelly, aboard a British merchant ship en route
from the West Indies to New York in 1782, thus described the "bays" trousers: "Here our master laid in
a few slops to sell us, from which each man was supplied with a pr. of red baize trousers, so that when we
were aloft reefing the sails we appeared like a flock of
flamingoes."[13]

During the early part of the century, grey and red
(grey jackets lined red and red vests) were the principal
colors of the Royal Navy.[14] Blue was introduced for
naval officers in 1748[15] and by the 1770s had become
the predominant color of British seamen's jackets. As
for American sailors of the Continental Navy, the
states' navies, the merchant service, and privateersmen,
color seemed to vary widely. Blue and brown jackets

7

Figure 5. *British Sailor, 1740-1780.*
From his dress, this sailor could either be a man-of-war's man
of the Royal Navy or a merchant seaman. His garments remained
characteristic of the British sailor for about forty years: round
hat cocked up on three sides; the ever-present kerchief, here
in a checked pattern (a striped pattern was also popular); a
striped waistcoat (sometimes also spotted or patterned, though
seldom checked); slops, or petticoat trousers, made of old sail
canvas (sometimes seen in either a checked or striped pattern);
and no shoes, which were often dispensed with in warm weather
aboard ship.
    Source: From "The Sailor's Return," in *The Dress of the
British Sailor* (London, 1957), courtesy of the National Maritime Museum. Drawing by author.

were the most common colors, but red, white, cloth-
colored, green, striped, and grey jackets were also worn.

The seaman's jacket was usually single-breasted and
embellished with metal, leather, or horn buttons. It
rarely had a collar or cape and was normally made
with slash cuffs, worn unbuttoned. Contemporary
pictures show that a few of these jackets were edged
with tape or lace. As early as 1706, some sailors' jackets
of the Royal Navy had "gold stitched button holes";
this style did not come into full vogue until a hundred
years later, during the Napoleonic period, when jackets
were often edged and decorated with white tape or
binding. This edging or binding was the exception during
the Revolutionary War.

Beneath the jacket most sailors wore an unlined
waistcoat or vest. The waistcoat was generally single-
breasted until the 1780s, after which it was more often
double-breasted or made with two rows of buttons
and cut straight across the bottom. With few exceptions, the vest had no pockets and was made of striped
cloth. While normally buttoned down the front, it was
occasionally tied with laces instead.

Under his vest, the sailor wore a body shirt, most
frequently made of checked linen. Around his neck
he wore a black kerchief, though colored kerchiefs
and checked or spotted ones in various colors were also
seen. In 1767, a Boston shopkeeper advertised "linen
checked, spotted, flowered, stamped, and bordered
cambrick, black gauze, yard wide handkerchiefs for
neckerchiefs." In some pictures of the period, the
shoregoing sailor is shown in a black or white cambric
stock or neck cloth such as gentlemen and soldiers wore.

Rough overgarments were worn when the men were
engaged in particularly heavy and dirty work aboard
ship. Hence, when his ship was beached on the Florida
coast in 1784, Samuel Kelly was barefoot and wore a
"shirt or canvas frock" while laboring at cleaning the
bottom of his vessel.[16] Several prints from the McPher-
son Collection of Naval Prints show sailors of the Royal
Navy wearing these canvas shirts while working the
guns in battle. The painting of Jan Willem DeWinter

surrendering to Adam, First Viscount Duncan at Camperdown in 1797 depicts several members of a gun crew aboard the HMS *Venerable* wearing long canvas shirts with slops.

The seafarer could choose among many styles of hat or cap. At sea, knitted hats and caps were the most popular because they served as the most practical attire on deck. Of this type, the knitted Monmouth cap, worn by sailors since the 1570s, had, by the eighteenth century, become the trademark of the English seaman. Ashore, many sailors liked the fashionable cocked hats, though the majority seemed to prefer the small round black hat made of a cheaper variety of felt or tarred canvas.[17] These round hats were often cocked up on three sides, a style that made the seamen look "as if they carried a triangular apple pastry upon their heads." heads."[18] When not cocked up, shoregoing hats were often adorned with a ribbon around the crown, knotted on one side or in front; the knot, a bow, was in the form of a cockade. The seamen liked to cock their hats rakishly over their eyes or push them onto the back of their heads.

American seamen, like their British cousins, also had a wide choice of headgear: leather caps, fur caps, cloth caps "turned up with fur" are all described as having been worn by the Americans. One sailor who deserted the Continental Navy was said to have a "gold laced cap." Another wore a "round hat, the crown painted red" as a means of waterproofing (a custom practiced by the U.S. merchant marine as recently as the 1940s). As shown in Hogarth's painting "An Election—Chairing the Member," circa 1754,[19] where a sailor has a hat with a red-painted crown, the British probably originated this custom. American seamen also wore "Dutch caps" and "Scotch bonnets." Sailors of the Royal Navy in the early eighteenth century wore "leather caps faced with red cotton."

Woolen gloves or mittens were listed in British naval stores for seamen as early as 1706. These items were issued to some soldiers in the Continental Army during the Revolution. American seamen of the eighteenth

Figure 6. *Navigation Officer in the Royal Navy, 1748.* Except for his cocked hat with loop and button which is that of a gentleman, his clothing is the same as that of the common seaman. Unlike most seamen's jackets which were made without pockets, this one has vertical pockets, a style more often seen in men's coats before 1750. Both his shirt and neckerchief are checked, and the end of his kerchief is tucked through his buttonhole, Steinkirk fashion. His trousers seem to be rather full, gathered in pleats at the waistband and terminating above the ankle. His small-buckled shoes are typical for the first half of the eighteenth century.

Source: From an advertisement for a maker of "mathematical instruments," "A New Sea Quadrant," invented and made by Geo. Adams, London, published 30 September 1748. Drawing by author.

9

Figure 7. *Master's Mate, Royal Navy, 1748.*
The Master, a warrant officer in the Royal Navy, was responsible for provisioning and fitting out a vessel for navigation when at sea. This Master's mate is shown with the navigation instruments of his trade. As a rated man, he is wearing the typical seaman's habit of the time. His trousers have a fall front, and his hat is cocked up fore and aft.
Source: From Dudley Jarrett, *British Naval Dress* (London, 1960). Drawing by author.

century had gloves or mittens, as did fishermen, for the purposes of protecting their hands against the elements.

As seen in contemporary illustrations, the shoes worn by seamen were almost always buckled. The shoe buckles, modest in size before 1750, became larger by 1785; this trend was in keeping with contemporary fashion. Laced shoes, only rarely seen on sailors, were most often worn by workers ashore. The footwear that the sailor purchased to wear ashore was apparently rather light and flimsy, but working shoes must have been sturdier to survive on deck. The *Continental Journal and Weekly Advertiser* of 27 August 1778 carried an advertisement for the Navy Board at Philadelphia: "Wanted, at the Navy Board, men's shoes, made well and strong, and also good yarn stockings; for which cash will be given at their office in Milk Street."

Seaboots, made of oiled leather and resembling the rubber seaboots worn by seamen today, were more common among fishermen than seamen, although one deserter from a French naval vessel in America in 1780 "carried with him a large pair of sailors boots." "Old Greenland boots" served as part of the gear of a British merchant seaman.[20]

Another item of clothing was the "great coat."

Samuel Kelly mentioned that he wore his "great coat" while on watch in the British packet service in 1781.[21] The great coat, or surtout coat, a large, loose overcoat reaching below the knees and cut straight in front, was worn by all social classes in the eighteenth century. A sailor is shown wearing one in Copley's "Watson and the Shark," a painting portraying an incident in Havana harbor in the 1760s. Hogarth painted a seafarer wearing a great coat in his picture of Lord George Graham in his cabin, circa 1750. Great coats, blue ones, were also issued in America: seamen of the *Scorpion* of the Virginia State Navy received them in 1776.[22]

While the perennial "pea jacket" is generally believed to have originated in the early nineteenth century, it is mentioned as having been worn by two runaway indentured servants in Pennsylvania in 1730. One jacket was described as being brown, double-breasted, with brass buttons and lined with red cloth. Further, a Negro deserter from an American vessel in 1778 is described as having worn a "surtout coat and a drab pea jacket under, and a pair of fearnaught trousers."[23] In a letter to Governor John Trumbull of Connecticut from Valley Forge in January 1778, George Washington described the pea jacket as it existed at that time: "I would recommend a garment of the pattern of the sailor's pea jacket, this sets close to the body, and by buttoning

Figure 8. *Lord George Graham in His Cabin, 1745.* Lord Graham, son of the Duke of Montrose, was a Captain in the Royal Navy. Here he is shown attended by a cabin boy dressed in a white apron, canvas trousers, neckerchief or neck cloth, and jacket and cap perhaps made of unbleached linen. The cabin boy serves the Captain's dinner wearing white cotton gloves. The Negro sailor entertaining the Captain with tamboreen and flute wears a cloth cap, neckerchief, watch coat, waistcoat, and trousers.

Source: "Lord George Graham in His Cabin," by William Hogarth, circa 1745; Milia Davenport, *The Book of Costume* (New York, 1948), vol. 2, p. 756; and "Portraits at the National Maritime Museum," Series 1, 1570-1748, London HMSO, 1954.

Figure 9. *British Seaman's Return, 1744.*
The seaman has returned to his love triumphant, loaded with spoils. He wears an "apple tasty" hat caught up on three sides, a gentleman's fine linen ruffled shirt, a waistcoat with gold binding, and a gentleman's knee breeches and stockings. Around his waist is a cutlass, and a pistol is thrust through his belt. He also sports a gold-beaded walking stick. In the midst of this sartorial finery, he continues to wear his distinctive sailor's jacket, hat, and kerchief.
Source: A print in the author's collection, entitled "The Sailor's Return," by J. Booth-Boitard, London, 1744.

double over the breast, adds much to the warmth of the soldier." The pea jacket, as seen in period illustrations, was merely a sailor's jacket of heavy cloth, made double-breasted and lined.

The weather called for functional clothing, especially against the cold winter winds at sea. The British seamen wore tarred clothing as protection against wet weather, a custom dating back to at least 1631.[24] They wore tarred canvas jackets and tarred canvas frocks as well. Tarring was also known in America. One American marine during the Revolution was described as wearing a "rifle frock, much tarred." He had taken his military-issue rifle frock and had tarred it against the weather for sea duty.[25] Other descriptions indicate that trousers, as well as hats and jackets, were sometimes tarred. A tarred, knitted hat with a brim all around—apparently of eighteenth-century origin— was recently discovered in a waterfront area of New York City.[26]

No discussion of the eighteenth-century seaman's dress would be complete without special mention of the shoregoing dress. Prints of the period occasionally show sailors in shoregoing finery (and usually swaggering in the company of flashy young women), their outfits patterned somewhat on those of the gentry. Samuel Kelly wrote of a trip ashore, "I had exchanged my old sea clothes for a fashionable blue coat, ruffled shirt, etc., with my hair dressed and powdered."[27] Hence, ruffled shirts, silver shoe buckles, tinsel-bound cocked hats, knee breeches, and swords are all very much in evidence. The sailor ashore sometimes wore a military coatee or short coat which was cuffed, caped, and lapeled in military fashion, with contrasting colored facings. He also affected the wearing of swords, usually short hangers or cutlasses, slung from a shoulder belt.

The American Seaman's Dress

Since there are so few pictures of American seamen of the eighteenth century, we must turn to other sources. Descriptions of deserters and runaways from vessels in American ports printed in Continental and colonial newspapers provide as exact a picture as can be found anywhere.

Two men who deserted in July 1776 from the *Hero* galley of the Virginia State Navy are thus described in the *Virginia Gazette:* "Charles Freeman . . . who had . . . a brown sailors jacket with an under jacket of scarlet stuff that had been turned, a check shirt, and a pr. of oznabrug trousers," and James Marten in "a brown sailor's jacket, a white linen shirt, oznabrug trousers and a new hat." On 20 September 1776, a deserter—boatswain's mate—was described to be wearing "a short coat of brown cloth and a red jacket." Clothing issues to the crew of the *Hero* confirm that the men were issued brown jackets, red waistcoats, and oznabrug trousers.[28] Three deserters from the *Liberty* brigantine of the Virginia State Navy in September 1776 were reported by the *Maryland Gazette* (26 September 1776) as wearing red jackets and oznabrug trousers. The same newspaper lists five deserters from the *Scorpion* sloop of war in August 1776, who had blue jackets and oznabrug trousers.[29]

A runaway sailor from the privateer sloop *Lyon* was described in the *Connecticut Gazette* in December 1776 as "one Samuel Smith junior, of Worthington, a parish of Middletown, . . . about 5 feet 10 inches high, dark complexion, has long black hair, had on when he went away, a redish surtout coat and striped trousers, with a blanket rolled round for a pack." The same newspaper in October 1776 described a deserter from the Connecticut Navy ship *Oliver Cromwell* as wearing "a short green jacket, striped trowsers, a small round hat, and a checked woolen shirt."

The narrative of a young sailor in 1781 provides us with another description of the American sailor's dress: "I stowed in my knapsack a thick woolen sailor jacket, well lined, a pair of thick pantaloons, one vest, two shirts, 2 pr. of stockings, one pr. of shoes, a pr. of heavy silver shoe buckles, a pair of knee buckles, two silk handkerchiefs." He also had a "small round hat," and the pewter buttons on his jacket bore the motto "Liberty and Property."[31]

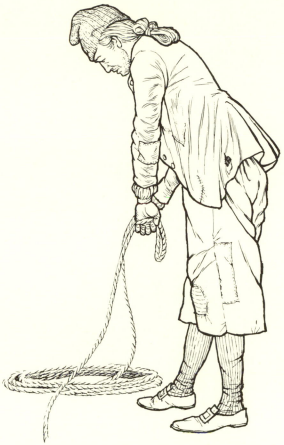

Figure 10. *Sailor's Working Dress, 1750-1770.*
This seaman, coiling a line on deck, wears the typical working dress of the 1750-1770 period: Monmouth cap; a simply made canvas jacket of old sailcloth, patched and repaired; sailcloth trousers, made very full; ribbed stockings; and shoes with simple pewter buckles. His hair, worn in a queue when ashore, is drawn up and clubbed with twine or rope yarn.
Source: Drawing by author from various sources.

Figure 11. *Peg-legged English Tar, 1754.*
This English tar, shown wielding his cudgel in a political brawl, is wearing a cocked hat edged with white tape or silver tinsel, the crown of which has been painted red. His neckerchief has a white polka dot pattern. His jacket has back and side vents, and his trousers are probably canvas.

Source: From an oil painting entitled "An Election—Chairing the Member," by William Hogarth, circa 1754, at Sir John Sloane's Museum, London; *Apollo Magazine,* January 1972: 6. Drawing by author.

Figure 12. *British Sailors Ashore, 1779.*
The shoregoing clothing worn by the seaman on the left was the style throughout most of the eighteenth century (1725-1800): round hat cocked up with a colored ribbon cockade, checked shirt, single-breasted waistcoat, neckerchief, and jacket. The seaman on the right wears the shorter jacket and straight-bottomed, double-breasted waistcoat which began to come into fashion around 1780. His jacket is edged with white tape binding, and the button holes are bound with white tape, again an embellishment that began to be seen around 1780. He also sports a striped kerchief.

Source: From "The Sailor's Pleasure," by Bowles and Carver, 1781, a drawing from *The Mariner's Mirror,* dated 1779; and Charles N. Robinson, *The British Tar in Fact and Fiction* (London, 1909). Drawing by author.

14

Figure 13. *American Sailors, 1776.*
These two sailors are from the brigantine *Liberty* of the Virginia State Navy. The drawing is based on descriptions published in the *Maryland Gazette* for 26 September 1776. One sailor is shown holding a deck scraper, and the other a tar brush.

    Source: From Williamsburg Public Store Daybook, Virginia Navy Board Minute Book, 26 March 1777-10 September 1778, Virginia State Library, Richmond, Virginia. Drawing by author.

Figure 14. *Carpenters at the Chicahominy Shipyard, Charles County, Virginia, 1778.*
In 1777-1778, the Navy Board issued the carpenters cotton strips (for making up trousers and jackets), as well as blue stroud, brown linen, hats, caps, and blankets. The Negro carpenter holds a "reaming beetle," an iron-bound wooden mallet used for caulking a ship's bottom; the other carpenter carries a lathing hatchet.

    Source: From Navy Board Orders in favor of shipyard workers, Williamsburg Public Store, Virginia State Library, Manuscript Collection. Drawing by author.

Figure 15. *Crew Member of an American Privateer, 1776.*
This privateersman wears typical seamen's dress. He is armed
with a cutlass, worn in a scabbard suspended from his waist
belt. A number of screw-barreled flintlock pistols complete his
adornment.
    Source: From a drawing, "Custavus Cunyingham, the
American Privateersman," Mariner's Museum, Newport News,
Virginia; and *American Heritage Book of the Revolution*
(New York, 1958), p. 292. Drawing by author.

Figure 16. *Sailor of the Continental Navy, 1776-1780.*
The round knitted hat is similar to one recently discovered
buried in the wreckage of a vessel of the period at Old Slip,
New York. The petticoat trousers are of old, patched sail cloth,
and the stockings are ribbed worsted, perhaps grey or light
blue. His jacket might be brown, green, grey, blue or red,
with black leather buttons. Drawing by author from various
sources.

16

Figure 18. *Sailors Afloat and Ashore.*
The view below is of British sailors aboard ship; above
shows them dressed for a night ashore. Both seafarers sport
short swords slung from shoulder belts when attired for shore.
One carries a cane or stock, and the other wears a ribbon in his
hat. Otherwise, their dress is identical: short jackets, straight-
bottomed vests without skirts, petticoat trousers, stockings,
light shoes, and neckerchiefs.

    Source: From a print entitled "Published as the Act Directs,
Nov. 8th, 1779 by W. Richardson, #68 High Holborn;"
initials of artist "I.P."; *Mariner's Mirror,* vol. 9.

Figure 17. *Sailors of the Gundello "Philadelphia," Lake
Champlain, 1776.*
The seamen shown here are dressed as typical working men
of the period. The two on the right have on seamen's jackets,
and the figure on the left a single-breasted, homespun coat.
The man on the far right wears Indian moccasins and a hat
cocked in old-fashioned style. The black sailor in the center
has been doing rope work, splicing and serving an eye about
a thimble.

    Source: From a drawing in the Military History Hall,
Museum of History and Technology, courtesy of The Smithsonian Institution, Washington, D.C. Drawing by author.

Figure 19. *Bostonians Tarring and Feathering a Tax Collector, 1773.*
The figure on the right is represented as a seaman. He would appear to be wearing a knitted hat, rather than a cap, and a spotted neckerchief.

   Source: A print in the author's collection, "The Boston Tea Party, 1773," by Philip Dawe.

18

281 **The SAILOR's PRESENT — or The JEALOUS CLOWN.**
From the Original Picture by John Collet, in the possession of Carington Bowles.
Printed for Carington Bowles, No 69 in St Pauls Church Yard London. Published as the Act directs

Figure 20. *English Seafarer, Circa 1775-1780.*
The sailor, with his small, round black hat edged with white
tape and fancy red ribbon cockade on the left side, is dressed
for a day ashore. His blue sailor's jacket and striped vest have
fine brass buttons. His trousers might be made of old, tarred,
tarpaulin canvas, which turns pale grey with age and becomes
quite thin, soft, and pliant. His stockings are striped in red and
white, and his shoes have brass buckles.
    Source: "The Sailor's Present—Or the Jealous Clown,"
after an original picture by John Collet, printed for Carrington
Bowles, London, undated.

Figure 21. *American Sailing Master, 1776-1781.*
The sailor's small, three-cornered hat, kerchief, jacket, and petticoat trousers are typical of the foremast hand of the latter part of the eighteenth century. His horizontally striped stockings are in the mode of the early 1780s.
   Source: Peter Copeland, *Everyday Dress of the American Revolution* (New York, 1975).

Figure 22. *The Virginia State Navy, 1776-1780.*
A group of Virginia seamen carouses at a waterfront tavern. They are from various vessels of the Virginia State Navy, and hence are clothed variously: *Diligence* galley, dark blue jackets, cloth-colored trousers, 1778; the ship *Dragon,* brown jackets and trousers, 1777-1778; the ship *Gloucester,* white baize jackets and trousers, 1777-1780; the brig *Northampton,* brown jackets with red facings, circa 1777; the sloop *Scorpion,* blue jackets and duck trousers, circa 1776.
   Source: Peter Copeland and Marko Zlatich, *Military Uniforms in America,* Plate 308, courtesy of the Company of Military Collectors and Historians.

Figure 23. *The "Hero" Galley, Virginia State Navy,*
1776-1778.
The men on the *Hero* were issued suits of clothing, described
in 1776 as follows: brown jackets, cloth-colored and striped
trousers, red vests, checked shirts, and grey yarn stockings.
The jackets had wooden buttons. Their headgear was various;
the man in the center wears a "Scotch bonnet."

   Source: Copeland and Zlatich, op. cit., Plate 251, courtesy
of the Company of Military Collectors and Historians.

Figure 24. *Seaman of a Continental Man-of-War, 1777.*
This seaman wears a jacket and trousers of mattress ticking,
a vest of striped wool, and a shirt of checked linen. He has
a small round felt hat, buckled shoes, and a neckerchief of
linen. Drawing by author.

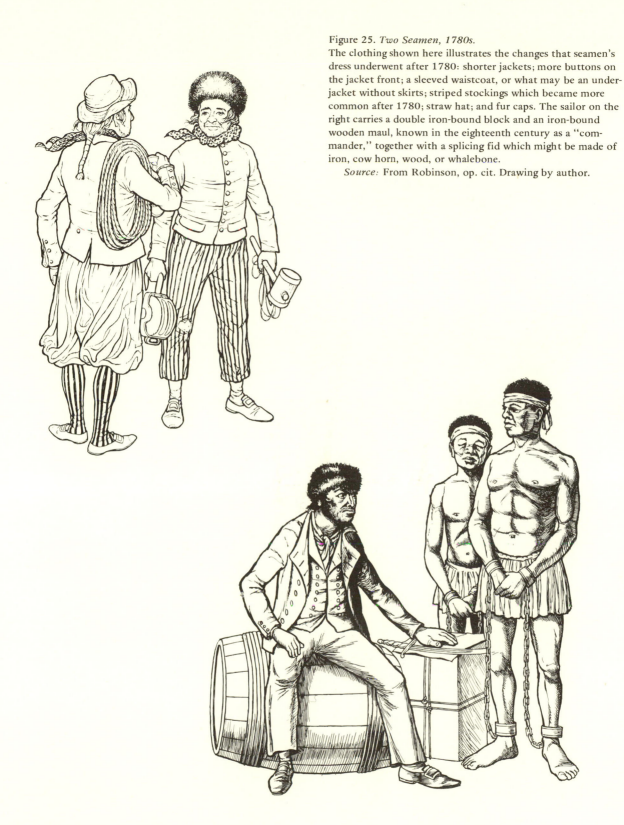

Figure 25. *Two Seamen, 1780s.*
The clothing shown here illustrates the changes that seamen's dress underwent after 1780: shorter jackets; more buttons on the jacket front; a sleeved waistcoat, or what may be an under-jacket without skirts; striped stockings which became more common after 1780; straw hat; and fur caps. The sailor on the right carries a double iron-bound block and an iron-bound wooden maul, known in the eighteenth century as a "commander," together with a splicing fid which might be made of iron, cow horn, wood, or whalebone.
Source: From Robinson, op. cit. Drawing by author.

Figure 26. *English Slaver, 1780.*
The seaman is dressed in period dress: jacket and trousers, double-breasted waistcoat, neckerchief, and fur cap. The edged weapon on the box is either a hunting sword or dirk.
Source: A watercolor by B. Reading, 1780, Liverpool Public Libraries; *History Today* (October 1972). Drawing by author.

23

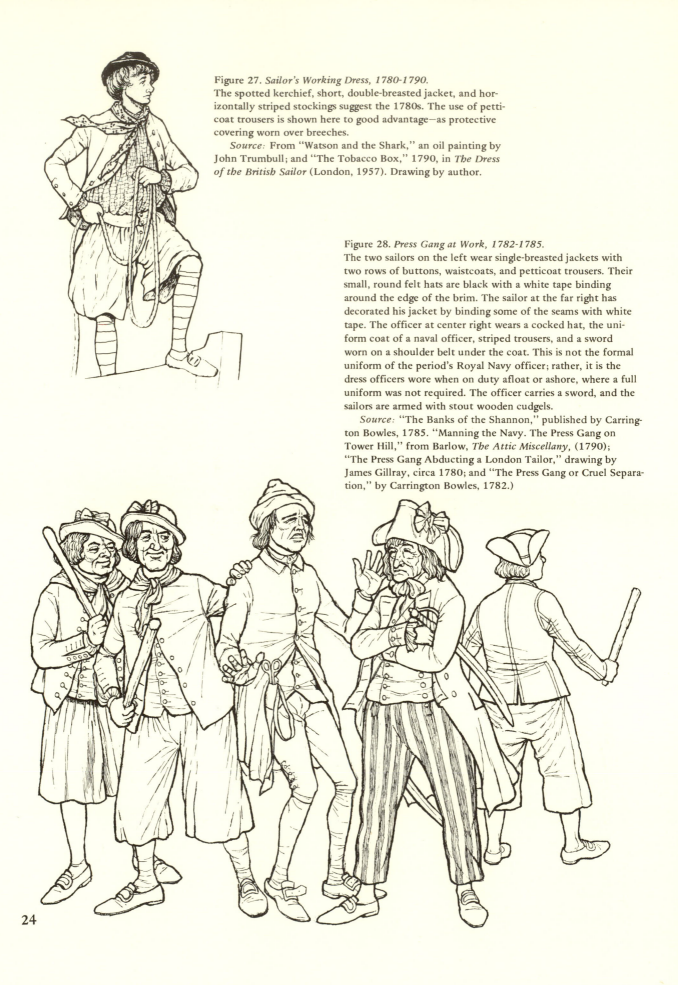

Figure 27. *Sailor's Working Dress, 1780-1790.*
The spotted kerchief, short, double-breasted jacket, and horizontally striped stockings suggest the 1780s. The use of petticoat trousers is shown here to good advantage—as protective covering worn over breeches.
   Source: From "Watson and the Shark," an oil painting by John Trumbull; and "The Tobacco Box," 1790, in *The Dress of the British Sailor* (London, 1957). Drawing by author.

Figure 28. *Press Gang at Work, 1782-1785.*
The two sailors on the left wear single-breasted jackets with two rows of buttons, waistcoats, and petticoat trousers. Their small, round felt hats are black with a white tape binding around the edge of the brim. The sailor at the far right has decorated his jacket by binding some of the seams with white tape. The officer at center right wears a cocked hat, the uniform coat of a naval officer, striped trousers, and a sword worn on a shoulder belt under the coat. This is not the formal uniform of the period's Royal Navy officer; rather, it is the dress officers wore when on duty afloat or ashore, where a full uniform was not required. The officer carries a sword, and the sailors are armed with stout wooden cudgels.
   Source: "The Banks of the Shannon," published by Carrington Bowles, 1785. "Manning the Navy. The Press Gang on Tower Hill," from Barlow, *The Attic Miscellany*, (1790); "The Press Gang Abducting a London Tailor," drawing by James Gillray, circa 1780; and "The Press Gang or Cruel Separation," by Carrington Bowles, 1782.)

Figure 29. *Sailor Ashore and Lady Friend, 1780-1785.*
The seaman wears a leather or felt cap trimmed with fur and a
checked kerchief knotted at his throat. His double-breasted
waistcoat and short jacket are typical of the 1780s.
   Source: Douglas Gorsline, *What People Wore*, New York,
1952). Drawing by author.

Figure 30. *Royal Navy Midshipman, 1785.*
The outfit shown here combines elements of sailor's and
officer's dress. His cocked hat and cockade, vest, coat (dark
blue faced with white with gilt buttons), and fine ruffled
shirt are those of a naval officer. He wears a sailor's neckerchief, however, and seaman's trousers instead of an officer's
breeches and stockings. As midshipmen were cadet officers,
their outfits usually resembled those of warrant officers of the
Royal Navy, though for formal dress affairs they wore the
naval officer's uniform.
   Source: Robinson, op. cit. Drawing by author.

Figure 31. *Officer of a Slave Ship, 1780-1785.*
This figure is drawn from a late eighteenth-century painting
depicting the capture of slaves on the West African coast.
From the ruffled shirt, long coat, and sword, it can be con-
jectured that he is a ship's officer. His sword has a brass hilt,
a black leather waistbelt, and scabbard. There is no indication
of nationality.
   Source: From a painting in the Rijksmuseum, Amsterdam;
Isabelle Agreet, *A Pictorial History of the Slave Trade* (Geneva,
1971). Drawing by author.

Figure 32. *American Seaman in Working Dress, 1785.*
Working aloft, this seaman wears a straw hat, neckerchief,
checked shirt, and patched, sailcloth trousers.
   Source: Drawing by author from various descriptions.

26

Figure 33. *American Ship's Carpenter and Officer, 1785.*
The carpenter wears a kerchief bound about his head, a checked
waistcoat, and a canvas apron tied at his waist with a bit of
ship's line. He has on a pair of laced shoes and no stockings.
  Source: Drawing by author from various descriptions.

27

Figure 34. *English Naval Cook, 1799.*
Men incapacitated in service were often employed as cooks aboard ship, for the cook's duties required less agility than those of a foremast hand. The cook shown here is wearing a simple cap, perhaps of coarse oznabrug linen, neckerchief, striped shirt, waistcoat, and a pair of slops.
   Source: From "A Naval Cook, 1799," a watercolor by T. Rowlandson; *The Dress of the British Sailor* (London, HMSO, 1957). Drawing by author.

Figure 35. *Royal Navy Carpenter, 1790.*
The carpenter wears a sleeveless waistcoat (with most of the buttons missing) and another underwaistcoat under it. His spotted kerchief is knotted tightly around his neck. His trousers have a fall front. His striped stockings and lightweight shoes with large buckles suggest the dress current from the mid-1780s through the 1790s.
   Source: From "Boiling the Pitch," by T. Rowlandson, 1799; *The Dress of the British Sailor.* Drawing by author.

28

Figure 36. *Royal Navy Gun Crew, 1790-1795.*
Four men in the gun crew are wearing smocks or shirts
(actually, overshirts as opposed to the body shirt which was
worn beneath the waistcoat or jacket). These smocks were
usually made of old sail canvas made smooth and soft with age.

   Source: From the painting "The Battle of Camperdown,"
MacPherson Collection. Drawing by author.

Figure 37. *Newfoundland Fishermen, 1715.*
The man in the foreground wears a hooded jacket and petticoat trousers. An apron, probably of canvas, is around his
waist and neck, and he carries a cod hook in his hand. The
background figure wears a hat much like the modern sou'
wester in shape, probably of tarpaulin; a coat and mittens;
and an apron to protect his front. Both fishermen have seaboots of oiled leather.
  Source: From a map of North America, 1715, in Herman
Moll, *Atlas Royal*, British Museum. Drawing by author.

part 2. The Fisherman

The British fisherman's working dress was nearly
identical to that of the sailor. Like the sailor, he too
wore petticoat and long trousers, jacket, cap, and gloves.
Drawings of both French and British fishermen show
that seaboots made of leather, coming up to above the
knee, were popularly worn as a protection against the
sea and rough weather. These boots were probably
"pegged," that is, the sole of the boot and the inner
sole were fastened together with wooden pegs, a type
of construction dating back to at least the sixteenth
century. The wooden shoe, or sabot, was also worn as
a work shoe, especially by the French and Netherlanders.
Some fishermen preferred to go barefoot.

The mittens of yarn, heavy cloth, or animal skins
worn by fishermen since the sixteenth century continued into the eighteenth century.[31] Another type
of glove was the "haling hands"; this was made of wool
or felt, its palms often lined with leather. Many fishermen wore tarpaulin or turned canvas leggings over
trousers, no doubt as safeguards from both the fish
and the water.

As for the American fishermen, we have this description of a harpooner on a Nantucket whaling vessel:
"He wears a jacket closely buttoned, and round his
head a handkerchief lightly bound; in his hand he holds
the dreadful weapon, made of the best steel.[32] We also
know that American fishermen wore "barvells" (coarse
leather aprons) while cleaning fish. One of the most
popular types of footwear among them was the "broags,"
which were coarse rawhide shoes with heavy soles tied
with a single lace.

The dress of the wives and daughters of fishermen
is also of interest for they worked alongside their men.
They cleaned and hauled the fish, made and repaired
nets, and prepared and sold the catch. These fisherwomen were attired much as other working women of
the period: corset-bodice, jacket, skirt, apron, and
coif or cap. These garments had changed very little

Figure 38. *French Fisherwomen of Dieppe, 1762.*
The girl on the left wears an open-necked bodice and a full
skirt made of coarse, heavy brown cloth reaching just below
the knee. On her head she wears a loose kerchief. As in many
pictures of French fisherwomen she is barefoot. The girl on
the right wears a soft hat probably made of unbleached linen,
a skirt, and a long jacket of a reddish cloth. Under the jacket
she wears an unbleached linen blouse.

Source: From Joseph Vernet's "Port of Dieppe," 1762,
Musée de la Marine, Paris; Alfred Cobban, ed., *The 18th
Century* (New York, 1969), p. 160. Drawing by author.

over the centuries and continued unchanged throughout
the eighteenth century. For example, the hooked corset-
bodice retained much the same form that it had had in
the sixteenth century.

In warm weather the women wore full-sleeved short
blouses under their corsets. The bodice was a separate
garment from the skirt so that it could be removed for
work in warm weather. A wide kerchief was often worn
over the bodice. The fashionable hoop skirts of the
gentry were not seen among working women.[33] Many
wore large white aprons made of heavy cotton (sometimes of canvas) and coarse petticoats.[34]

Most of the women went barefoot. When shoes were
worn, they were often wooden sabots among French
fisherwomen and wooden pattens raised on iron rings
among the English. English fisherwomen also wore the
short leather shoes (square-toed, either buckled or tied)
commonly worn by working women of the time.[35]

These fisherwomen usually wore simple mob caps,
the normal head covering of the lower class woman.
Broad-brimmed, flat-crowned hats were also common.

31

Figure 39. *French Fisherman of Dieppe, 1762.*
This fisherman is seen carrying his catch in wicker baskets to market. He wears a cloth cap of unbleached material, perhaps coarse linen. His trousers appear to be of brown cloth or canvas, and his boots are of oiled leather.
  Source: From Joseph Vernet's "Port of Dieppe"; Cobban, op. cit., p. 160. Drawing by author.

Figure 40. *French Cod Fisherman and Wife, 1769.*
The fisherman wears a small, battered, round hat, perhaps made of tarpaulin canvas, an ordinary workman's jacket, and sabots. Over his trousers is a legging (perhaps of tarred canvas), a form of protection cheaper than seaboots. His wife wears a flat-topped, round hat, probably of castor or cheap felt. A jacket tucked into her skirt affords protection from the weather. She wears slippers and pattens, more often seen among English working men and women than among the French.
  Source: From M. Duhamel du Monceau, *Traité Général des Pesches et Histoire des Poissons* (Paris, 1769-1777); *Album of American History* (Colonial Period), 1944. Drawing by author.

Figure 41. *American Fisherman, 1776.*
The jacket, trousers, knitted Monmouth cap, and kerchief
are those of the seafarer. His seaboots are of heavy leather with
wood-pegged soles. Under his jacket is a coarse linen body
shirt. He carries a heaving line and boat hook.
    Source: Copeland, op. cit.

Figure 42. *Boston Fishmonger, 1744.*
The fishmonger wears a striped jacket, double-breasted waistcoat, canvas apron, and buckled shoes. His small round hat is of
black felt with an edging of white tape, and his trousers are of
red baize. The buttons on his jacket are made of lead. He carries
a wooden shovel for loading baskets of fish.
    Source: Copeland, *Everyday Dress of the American Revolu-
tion,* based on a contemporary cartoon entitled "Bostonians
in Distress," 1744, Chicago Historical Society.

Figure 43. *Gay Head Indian, Harpooner, 1780.*
Many of these Indians sailed in the ships of the American whaling fleet. In his book, *Journal of Occurrences of the Late American War,* Roger Lamb describes the dress of a Nantucket harpooner aboard a Yankee whale ship: "He wears a jacket closely buttoned, and round his head a handkerchief lightly bound; in his hands he holds the dreadful weapon, made of the best steel . . . to the shaft of which the end of a cord is firmly tied."
Source: Copeland, op. cit.

Figure 44. *Scottish Fisherwoman, 1792.*
Colored kerchief knotted under her chin over what appears to be a coif or close-fitting undercap; heavy, woolen, striped overskirt bunched up about her waist; shawl perhaps of tartan cloth; and petticoat of stout material and of a bright color with stripes.
Source: From "Series of English Portraits," by John Kay, 1838, Edinburgh; Alma Oakes and Margot H. Hill, *Rural Costume* (London, 1970), p. 176. Drawing by author.

Figure 45. *French Fisherman, 1801.*
The dress of this old fisherman was not much different from that of the average French working man of 1730-1810. The Phrygian cap, worn by workers all over Europe for many centuries, was known during the American Revolution as the "Liberty Cap." The leggings are perhaps made of tarred canvas.
Source: From the painting "Port of Dieppe" by Joseph Vernet. Drawing by author.

Figure 46. *Whalers of a Greenland Fishery, 1744.*
The jackets and full breeches seen here are similar to the garments worn by Dutch seamen of the period. The fisherman
in the rear wears sailor's petticoat trousers and a form of leggings.
The man on the right has on leather seaboots and carries a har-
poon, one of several types of whaling harpoons used.
    Source: From Monck's *Account of a Most Dangerous Voyage
to Greenland,* in Churchill's *Voyages, London 1744,* vol. 1,
p. 54; Kendall Museum Whaling Prints, by M. V. and Dorothy
Brewington, Kendall Whaling Museum, Sharon, Massachusetts,
1969. Drawing by author.

Figure 47. *English Fisherfolk, 1810.*
Two of the fishermen shown are wearing caps made of cloth,
or knitted Monmouth caps. Two of the fishermen are wearing
leather boots. The woman's round hat is pulled down over a cap.
    Source: From William H. Pyne, *Microcosm* (London, 1806).
Drawing by author.

Figure 48. *French Whalers, 1780s.*

Single-breasted jackets, waistcoats, trousers and full breeches, round hats, and fur caps such as these were commonly worn by whalers during this period. The man on the left wears his waistcoat or underjacket tucked into his full, loose breeches.

Source: From M. Duhamel du Monceau, *Traité Generale des Pesches et Histoire des Poissons* (Paris, 1782); *Kendall Whaling Museum Prints,* Kendall Whaling Museum (Sharon, Massachusetts, 1969), p. 187; Leonard Harrison Mathews, *The Whale* (New York, 1968), p. 118. Drawing by author.

NOTES

1. Charles H. Sherrill, *French Memories of 18th Century America* (New York, 1915).
2. Carl Bridenbaugh, *Cities in Revolt: Urban Life in America, 1743-1776* (New York, 1955), p. 86.
3. Jesse Lemisch, "Jack Tar in the Streets," *William and Mary Quarterly* (July 1968): 378.
4. Ibid.
5. Bridenbaugh, op. cit., p. 309.
6. Lemisch, op. cit., p. 395.
7. Library of Congress, Manuscript Division, Record Group 94.
8. *Pennsylvania Gazette* (January 1729).
9. *Society for Army Historical Research,* Vol. 10 (London, 1931), p. 125.
10. C. Lloyd and L. S. Coulter, *Medicine and the Navy, 1200-1900,* Vol. 3, 1714-1815 (London and Edinburgh, 1961), p. 77.
11. Peter Copeland and Marko Zlatich, *Military Uniforms in America,* Plate 308: "The Virginia State Navy."
12. Description of a deserter from the brig *Liberty,* Virginia State Navy, 1776, Company of Military Historians (1968).
13. Samuel Kelly, *Samuel Kelly, An Eighteenth Century Seaman* (New York, 1925), p. 97.
14. Dudley Jarrett, *British Naval Dress* (London, 1960), pp. 15-30.
15. Cunnington, Lucas, and Mansfield, *Occupational Costume in England,* p. 59.
16. Samuel Kelly, op. cit.
17. *Williamsburg Day Book,* 13 June 1776, Virginia State Library, Richmond, Virginia. Courtesy of Marko Zlatich.
18. "The Dress of the British Sailor," National Maritime Museum (London, 1957).
19. "John Sloan's Museum," *Apollo Magazine* (January 1972): 7.
20. Samuel Kelly, op. cit.
21. Ibid., p. 29.
22. *Williamsburg Day Book,* 22 June 1776, Virginia State Library, Richmond, Virginia.
23. *Pennsylvania Ledger,* 15 April 1778. Courtesy of Albert W. Haarmann.
24. Charles N. Robinson, *The British Tar in Fact and Fiction* (London, 1909), p. 97.
25. *New York Journal No. 1776,* 8 September 1777.
26. Personal communication from Don Troiani, July 1970.
27. Samuel Kelly, op. cit.
28. Copeland and Zlatich, *Military Uniforms in America,* Plate 251: "The *Hero* Galley, Virginia State Navy, 1776-1778."

Figure 49. *Young English Waterman, 1792.*
The waterman poles a punt along a river for some gentlemen anglers. Except for his trousers, which are a bit fuller and longer than those worn earlier in the century, he appears in typical seaman's clothing of the 1770s and 1780s.

    Source: A print in the author's collection, entitled "Patience in a Punt," by W. Dickinson, London, 1792.

29. Ibid., Plate 308: "The Virginia State Navy."
30. *The Adventures of Christopher Hawkins* (New York, 1864). Courtesy of Jane Ross.
31. Cunnington, Lucas, and Mansfield, op. cit., pp. 54-57.
32. Roger Lamb, *Journal of Occurrences of the Late American War* (Dublin, 1809), p. 203.
33. Alma Oakes and Margot H. Hill, *Rural Costume* (London, 1970), pp. 67-75.
34. Cunnington, Lucas, and Mansfield, op. cit., p. 64.
35. Oakes and Hill, op. cit., p. 81.

(2)
Farmers and
Rural Workers

Agriculture in the New World, originally serving only to keep the European settlers alive, expanded so phenomenally during the colonial period that, by the beginning of the eighteenth century, it had already become the vital link in America's trade activities. By this time, the agricultural goods produced in each group of colonies so far exceeded home consumption needs that they were regularly exported from colony to colony and abroad to England, the Continent, and the West Indies. The specialization practiced by each of the colonies encouraged this trade. New England with grazing and meat production, the middle colonies with grain production, and the South with tobacco, rice, indigo, and naval stores contributed heavily to America's growing capitalism during the 1700s.

As for the American farm worker, his condition was apparently better than that of European rural people. In 1782, the Abbé Robin observed: "These farmers, simpler than our peasants, have neither the rusticity nor the boorishness of the latter; better educated, they have neither their wilfulness nor their dissimulation. They are less hampered by ancient custom, and more ingenious in perfecting and inventing that which increases their comfort."[1] One factor which may have made the American less "rustic" was his closer ties with the city. A network of roads was built between farm and urban communities during the eighteenth century, primarily to answer the seaboard cities' needs for a trade outlet for their European imports.[2]

RURAL DRESS

With the end of serfdom and the abolition of the old sumptuary laws, the lot of rural people in England had improved considerably by the eighteenth century. To some degree, their dress reflected their improved fortunes. More and more their dress began to resemble that of urban workers. For example, they no longer wore aprons in the fields, and they now adopted the fashionable long coat.[3]

Not surprisingly, the colonial farmers, being removed

Figure 1. *German Peasant Woman, Circa 1720.*
This style of dress—tight-fitting cap, laced corset-bodice, and apron—was also that of German farm women in early eighteenth-century Pennsylvania.

    Source: From Oakes and Hill, *Rural Costume.* Drawing by author.

from Europe by only a generation or two, duplicated the dress worn in England. They too sought a model for their clothing among the urban population, though rural fashions usually lagged behind urban fashions by some years. The women, who made almost all of the rural work clothes, copied the styles of dress seen along most of the North Atlantic corridor.

With the multiplicity of nationalities in America, not all farmers dressed in the English style. Dutch fashions (as well as language) persisted in parts of New York State until the Revolution. In some sections of Pennsylvania, some German women dressed in the style of their mother country, and Scottish highland dress was seen in the back country of North Carolina as late as the 1770s. Largely, however, American farm dress closely resembled that of their rural cousins in Britain.

By midcentury, most rural men had abandoned the baggy breeches and loose jackets of the early 1700s, and their normal attire now consisted of the tight breeches and close-bodied, rather long-skirted jackets with many buttons of the type worn by urban workers and seamen. By the time the American Revolution began, many farmers had adopted the long, single-breasted frock coat then worn by all social classes. Farmers could now afford to wear waistcoats similar to those of city people, and many wore tight-fitting breeches like those of the gentry. The breeches came down over the knees and were fastened by buttons and buckles at the knee.[4] They were usually made of leather, deerskin, or sheepskin.[5]

40

Figure 2. *Irish Peasant Woman, 1710.*
This dress is typical of that worn by the Irish and Scots-Irish who colonized New Jersey and New York during the seventeenth century.
Source: From *American Heritage History of the Thirteen Colonies* (New York, 1967). Drawing by author.

The usual working dress for men in the fields consisted of a coarse linen shirt or smock with full-length sleeves and coming down to the knees; homespun trousers or breeches; a large uncocked, felt hat; and sturdy leather shoes. In hot weather, the plantation and farm workers wore skilts—short brown trousers that came just below the knees—rather than the uncomfortable tight-fitting breeches. The skilts were made of coarse tow cloth and in the South of "negro cloth" or "native-cloth."[6] Their shoes were sometimes girded around the heel with an iron strap, in the shape of a horse shoe. They were most often of the lace-up type, though with increasing affluence buckled shoes were by no means uncommon among rural folk. The wooden sabots worn by the farm people of Holland and France were not often seen in America. Indian moccasins were used by both sexes, especially in remote frontier areas. Short canvas or coarse linen gaiters, strapped or buttoned on the outer side of the leg, were also worn.

The Phrygian (or Saxon) cap, in much evidence in northern Europe, was also worn by American farmers. All classes of farm labor in England wore wigs, and, while popular in America as well, the custom was not as widespread there.

Farm women dressed in the style of urban working women. The basic garments were the corset-bodice, jacket, skirt, apron, and mob cap. As was the case in Europe, when farm women lived near a town their dress increasingly began to resemble that of the town women. In summer they usually wore a short-sleeved shirt or

Figure 3. *English Country Couple, Circa 1750.*
The farm boy wears a small cocked hat, sleeved waistcoat or jacket, and breeches with a fly front rather than the equally common fall front. His shoes are buckled, as are the lady's. She wears a mob cap of linen, a kerchief, simple dark dress, and apron probably of coarse linen.
   Source: From Robert Raines, *Marcellus Laroon* (London, 1966). Drawing by author.

blouse, with a kerchief about their necks and tucked into their corsets or bodices. Their aprons were made of linen or cotton and were colored, white, or checked. Many wore either a black or red hooded traveling cloak on a journey to town, or simply a man's surtout or great coat.

Both sexes wore wooden pattens with iron runners in wet weather. The women's stockings were knitted, usually in dark colors.

In both Scotland and England, many farm women wore simple kerchiefs over their heads and knotted under the chin, rather than hats or caps; this practice was probably followed in America as well. Flat, straw hats were seen in summer. Perhaps most rural women, however, favored a man's round felt hat when working outside. This wide-brimmed hat, called a "bullycock" in England, was very popular throughout rural America.

When working in the fields, some women did not wear a gown. A contemporary description from the late 1780s describes English farm women thus: "They have stays half laced and something by way of handkerchief about their necks; they wear a single coloured flannel or stuff petticoat, no shoes or stockings . . . and their coat [petticoat] is pinned up in the shape of a pair of trousers leaving them naked to the knee."[7] Apparently, many women abandoned the gown because it interfered with their efficiency while laboring in the fields. It was also common for farm women to wear men's clothing when doing outdoor work. Functional, loose clothing, to shelter one from the weather, marked the attire of all the rural folk at work.

42

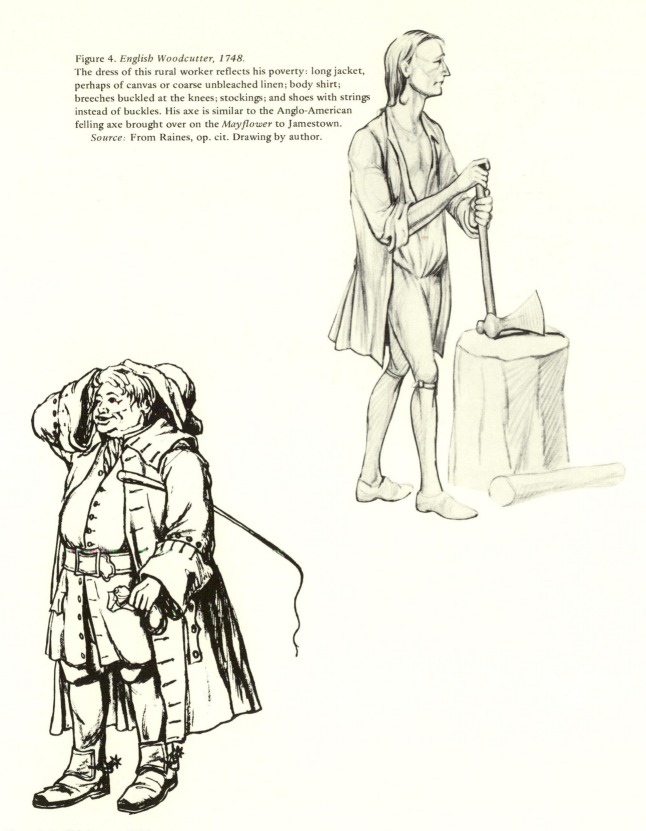

Figure 4. *English Woodcutter, 1748.*
The dress of this rural worker reflects his poverty: long jacket, perhaps of canvas or coarse unbleached linen; body shirt; breeches buckled at the knees; stockings; and shoes with strings instead of buckles. His axe is similar to the Anglo-American felling axe brought over on the *Mayflower* to Jamestown.
Source: From Raines, op. cit. Drawing by author.

Figure 5. *English Farmer, 1731.*
For his traveling dress, this farmer wears a broad-brimmed felt hat and a surtout with vertical pockets and the large cuffs of the time. He has a belted, single-breasted coat below the surtout, breeches, and large leather boots with spurs.
Source: From Raines, op. cit. Drawing by author.

43

Figure 6. *English Peasants at a Tavern, 1742.*
This rollicking group is in mixed dress. The two figures in the
background at the extreme left and right wear linen caps and
sleeveless waistcoats over short-sleeved underjackets. All of the
men except the fiddler wear short, close-cropped hair, suggesting
that all wore wigs habitually, even, presumably, at work.
  Source: From Raines, op. cit. Drawing by author.

Figure 7. *Old English Peasant, 1750.*
This old countryman wears a very battered, light-colored felt
hat, a tattered linen body shirt gathered up and knotted at the
waist, a surtout, breeches, leggings, and leather shoes fastened
with thongs or twigs.
  Source: From "Old Peasant with Donkey," an oil on canvas
by Thomas Gainsborough, owned by Mrs. H. W. Standring.
Drawing by author.

Figure 8. *Betrothal of Rustic French Peasants, 1761.*
The elderly man seated still wears his stockings pulled up over
the knees of his breeches in the fashion of the early part of
the century. As can be seen here, the dress of French rural
folk was much like that of English farm people of the time.
   Source: "Accordee de Village," an oil on canvas by Jean
Baptiste Greuze, 1761.

Figure 9. *English Farm Laborer, Circa 1770.*
He wears a large, round felt hat, single-breasted jacket, short
waistcoat without skirts, breeches, no stockings, and buckled
shoes. Many such men became indentured servants in the
American colonies.

   Source: From *American Heritage History of the Thirteen
Colonies.* Drawing by author.

Figure 10. *English Country Girl, 1770-1780.*
The striped kerchief above the bodice, long full apron pleated
at the waist, buckled shoes, and cap tied beneath the chin with
a ribbon were the typical clothes for young girls during the
latter half of the eighteenth century.

   Source: From A. P. Oppé, *The Drawings of Paul and Thomas
Sandby in the Collection of His Majesty the King at Windsor
Castle* (Oxford, 1947). Drawing by author.

Figure 11. *English Reaper, 1795.*
This worker presents an unusually neat appearance: sparkling white linen shirt, spotless breeches, and stockings as elegant as those of a gentleman.

    Source: From "Reapers," a painting by George Stubbs, circa 1795, in "Painting in England, 1700-1850," collection of Mr. and Mrs. Paul Mellon, Virginia Museum of Fine Arts. Drawing by author.

Figure 12. *German Farmer, 1773.*
Round hat cocked up on one side with a botton and loop, surtout with vertical slash pockets, breeches, stockings and buckled shoes.

    Source: From Daniel Chodowieckis, *Künstlerfahrt nach Danzig im Jahre 1773* (Berlin, 1908). Drawing by author.

Figure 13. *German Peasant Woman, 1773.*
The sacque dress, apron, and mob cap of this German woman from the area near Danzig closely resembles the dress of the colonial worker.

    Source: From Chodowieckis, op. cit. Drawing by author.

Figure 14. *Colonial Housewife, 1775.*
Beribboned mob cap, spotted bodice with kerchief tucked
into it, heavy woolen skirt, and apron made of mattress ticking.
   Source: Copeland, *Everyday Dress of the American
Revolution.*

Figure 15. *Colonial Farmer and Wife, 1776.*
The farmer wears a homespun jacket, waistcoat, and trousers;
small round felt hat; oznabrug linen apron; and Indian moccasins.
His wife has on a man's felt hat, surtout coat, and linen apron
over her skirt.
   Source: Copeland, op. cit.

Figure 16. *Colonial Milkmaid, 1777.*
Linen cap, spotted bodice, cotton blouse, coarse linen apron,
and well-worn homespun cloth skirt.
    Source: Copeland, op. cit.

Figure 17. *Colonial Shepherd, 1775.*
The long surtout coat resembles the sentry's watch coat worn
by soldiers of the time. The broad-brimmed hat gives good
protection from the elements. Beneath his coat the shepherd
wears a coarse linen shirt or smock. His breeches are of leather
and his stockings of ribbed worsted. He wears gaiters, or
"spatterdashes," commonly worn by laborers and soldiers in
the field. He carries a haversack for his food and a soldier's
tin canteen.
    Source: Copeland, op. cit.

49

Figure 18. *English Shepherd, Circa 1800.*
He wears the farmer's typical long, loose, linen smock, leather breeches, and gaiters. His food is carried in a tow-cloth haversack over his shoulder.
   Source: From William Henry Pyne, *Microcosm* (London, 1806). Drawing by author.

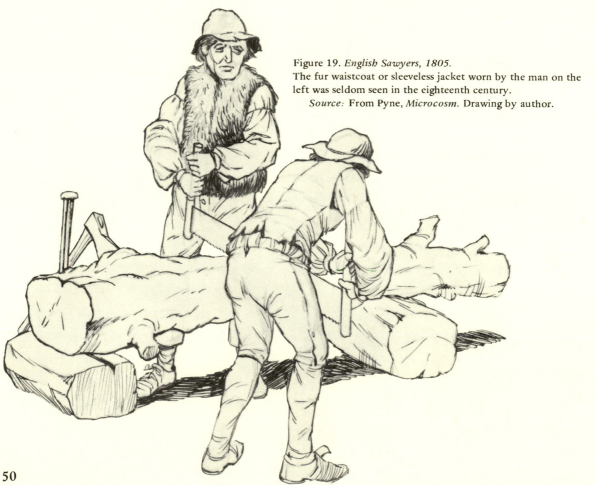

Figure 19. *English Sawyers, 1805.*
The fur waistcoat or sleeveless jacket worn by the man on the left was seldom seen in the eighteenth century.
   Source: From Pyne, *Microcosm.* Drawing by author.

50

Figure 21. *Rural Englishman, Circa 1810.*
Working man's round hat, kerchief, jacket, waistcoat, breeches, and canvas or coarse linen short leggings.
   Source: From William Henry Pyne, *Etchings of Rustic Figures* (London, 1814). Drawing by author.

Figure 20. *English Dairyman and Woman, 1805.*
This couple wears the typical farm dress of the time: The man has on a coarse linen (or tow) smock and short leggings; the woman wears a mob cap and an apron with a kerchief tucked loosely into her bodice.
   Source: From Pyne, *Microcosm.* Drawing by author.

Figure 22. *English Farm Woman, 1810*.
The round felt hat was the most common form of headgear
worn by rural people, both men and women, throughout the
American colonies.
  Source: From Pyne, *Etchings of Rustic Figures*. Drawing
by author.

52

Figure 23. *English Country Woman and Her Children, 1810*.
From the time they could walk, the children of working class
people wore the same kind of clothing as their parents.
  Source: From Pyne, *Etchings of Rustic Figures*. Drawing
by author.

Figure 24. *English Mowers, 1810.*
The mowers are seen carrying scythes into the field and a swiggett for carrying water or beer. The man on the right has at his waist a leather sheath for his sharpening stone.
    Source: From Pyne, *Microcosm.* Drawing by author.

NOTES

1. Sherrill, *French Memories of 18th Century America.*
2. Warwick, Pitz, and Wyckoff, *Early American Dress:* p. 147.
3. Cunnington, Lucas, and Mansfield, *Occupational Costume in England,* p. 30.
4. Ibid., p. 47.
5. Warwick, Pitz, and Wyckoff, op. cit., p. 159.
6. Earle, *Two Centuries of Costume in America,* pp. 764-765.
7. Ibid., p. 409.

(3)
Craftsmen and
Urban Workers

By the eighteenth century, the economy of colonial America was expanding rapidly. The colonists were now producing many goods domestically and were thereby relying less and less on the mother country. Since colonial industry was largely urban, an urban work force grew to service its needs.

Each group of colonies became more specialized in its industry as the century progressed, and, concomitantly, the labor force began to take on distinct regional characteristics. In the South, where agriculture predominated, an unskilled labor force composed mainly of black slaves arose. Except in Charleston, craftsmen were in short supply in the rural South[1] and remained scarce throughout the century. Whatever artisans there were primarily were blacks trained in the areas of carpentry, bricklaying, and the like; thus, the slaves supplanted the indentured servants who had filled these needs in the 1600s.[2] The slave artisans working on the plantations produced most of the manufactured goods required in the southern economy. Rural southern families, both rich and poor, made many articles on their own farms. The more affluent planters, using tobacco as the trading commodity, imported from England whatever goods could not be produced on their plantations. As a consequence, the southern colonies did not develop the class of "mechanics," or the system of apprenticeship into the crafts system, that loomed so large in the life of the northern colonies.

In the middle colonies, where urban communities were rapidly developing, and in New England, there was a heavy demand for skilled labor. Hence, the craftsman became an important member of the labor force. In contrast to the situation in the South, the northern colonies attracted a number of ethnic groups, who brought with them from Europe a knowledge of crafts and artisanship.

The mixture of English, Irish, Scots, French, Dutch, Germans, and Swedes that peopled the North was instrumental in creating and sustaining the boom in crafts throughout the eighteenth century. At the beginning of the Revolution, most clothing, particularly in rural

Figure 1. *French Printer, 1760s.*
Linen or cloth cap, jacket, or short, single-breasted coat, waist-coat, and bibbed apron fastened at the breast with string and button.
　　Source: From Denis Diderot, *Diderot's Pictorial Encyclopedia of Trades and Industry* (New York, 1959). Drawing by author.

areas, was still being manufactured at home, but a clothing industry was already expanding in the North. Silversmiths were flourishing by midcentury, and clock-making, begun in Connecticut in the early 1700s, was well known by the 1770s. Other prospering industries in the North included pottery, glass making, iron and brass welding, paper making, wig making, shoe making, tailoring and cloth making, hat making, cabinet making, coopering, shipbuilding, wagon and coach making, and leather working.

URBAN DRESS

In dress American urban workers tended very much to resemble their counterparts in Europe, except that in America they were somewhat more affluent and hence better attired. With their greater means and their daily commerce with the middle class, they were in a better position to copy the fashions of the day than rural workers were. Thus, urban workers and crafts-men wore their hair curled at the side in emulation of the upper class. They also wore cocked hats, stocks, ruffled shirts, buckled shoes, and coats rather than the jackets and smocks popular with the rural population.

The item of dress that probably most closely identi-fied the urban worker and craftsman as such was his apron. For example, in a description found in a pam-phlet entitled *Observations of the 4th of July, Grand Federal Procession, Philadelphia, 1788,* bread and bis-cuit makers wore "full plaited aprons" tied around the waist with a blue sash; gunsmiths, green baize aprons; curriers and tallow chandlers, blue aprons; cordwainers and coopers, white leather aprons; cabinet and chair makers, linen aprons.[3] Indeed, except for their aprons—and, of course, their tools and the quality of their clothing—there was little to distinguish them as crafts-men and urban workers.

Figure 2. *English Tinker, Circa 1785.*
The tinker was a craftsman at mending iron, brass, copper, tin, and pewter utensils. He wears a small round hat cocked up, sailor-style, jacket, breeches, and leather apron. His leather portmanteau containing the tools of his trade is slung over his back.
    Source: From *Catchpenny Prints,* by Bowles and Carver (London, 1970). Drawing by author.

Figure 3. *Colonial Carpenter, 1777.*
The carpenter depicted here—a free black man from New Jersey—wears a cocked hat, green cloth jacket, buff waistcoat, oznabrug linen trousers, and string-tied shoes. He wears no stockings.
    Source: Copeland, *Everyday Dress of the American Revolution.*

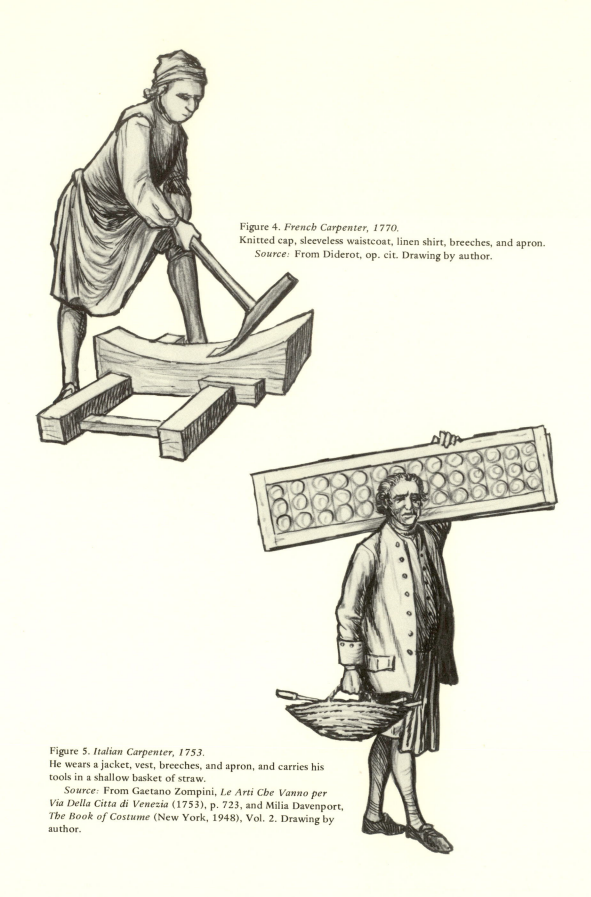

Figure 4. *French Carpenter, 1770.*
Knitted cap, sleeveless waistcoat, linen shirt, breeches, and apron.
Source: From Diderot, op. cit. Drawing by author.

Figure 5. *Italian Carpenter, 1753.*
He wears a jacket, vest, breeches, and apron, and carries his
tools in a shallow basket of straw.
   Source: From Gaetano Zompini, *Le Arti Che Vanno per
Via Della Citta di Venezia* (1753), p. 723, and Milia Davenport,
The Book of Costume (New York, 1948), Vol. 2. Drawing by
author.

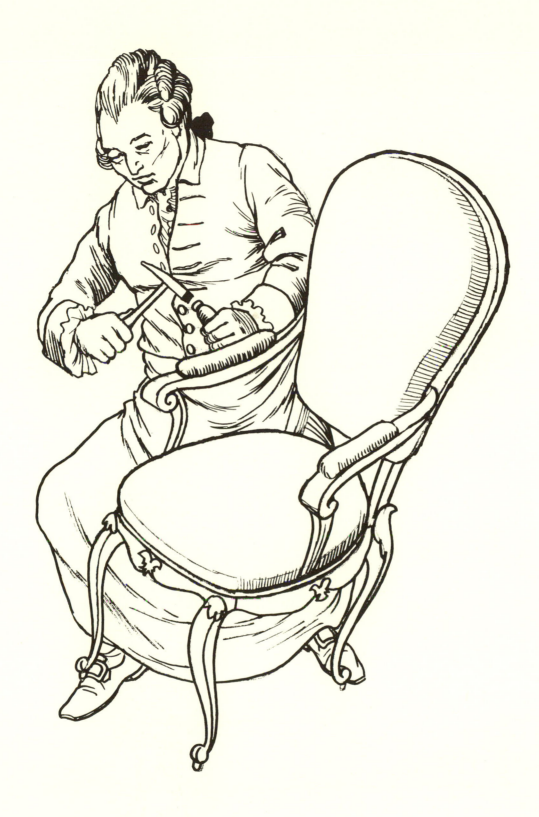

Figure 6. *French Cabinet Maker, 1762.*
Hair dressed and curled at the sides and tied up behind with a
ribbon in middle-class fashion, ruffled shirt, single-breasted
coat, apron, and buckled shoes.
  Source: From Diderot, op. cit. Drawing by author.

Figure 7. *American Wheelwright, 1788.*
Small round hat, jacket, leather breeches that tie at the knee, stockings, Indian-style moccasins, and leather apron tied with tongs at the waist.
  Source: Copeland, op. cit.

Figure 8. *American Cooper, Late 1770s.*
Linen cap, neckerchief, checked waistcoat, leather apron, leather breeches, linen shirt, and ribbed worsted stockings.
  Source: Copeland, op. cit.

Figure 9. *French Stonemason's Apprentice, 1760s.*
He is bareheaded, and he wears a sleeveless waistcoat, linen
body shirt, and leather breeches.
    Source: From Diderot, op. cit. Drawing by author.

Figure 10. *French Tinsmith, 1760s.*
Cap (probably knitted), double-breasted coat, shirt, and
breeches.
    Source: From Diderot, op. cit. Drawing by author.

Figure 11. *French Farrier and Apprentice, 1760s.*
The farrier wears a waistbelt with leather pouches which con-
tain his tools; a jacket with the sleeves cut off above the elbow;
and a leather apron. His apprentice wears a cap, double-breasted
waistcoat, and leather apron. Both men have slippers instead
of shoes.
    Source: From Diderot, op. cit. Drawing by author.

61

Figure 12. *American Smith, 1779.*
Linen cap, working man's jacket, checked shirt, ragged leather apron, worsted stockings, cloth slippers, and black leather breeches.
   Sources: Copeland, op. cit.

Figure 13. *French Blacksmith, 1760s.*
Cocked hat, bibbed apron, jacket, breeches, and buckled shoes.
Source: From Diderot, op. cit. Drawing by author.

Figure 14. *English Coppersmith, 1805.*
Short jacket beneath a sleeveless waistcoat, striped shirt, kerchief, breeches unbuckled at the knee, and buckled shoes.
   Source: From Pyne, *Microcosm.* Drawing by author.

Figure 15. *French Pewterer, 1788.*
Cocked hat, sleeved waistcoat, apron, and breeches.
   Source: From Pierre-Augustin Salmon, *L'art du Potier d'Etain* (Paris, 1788). Drawing by author.

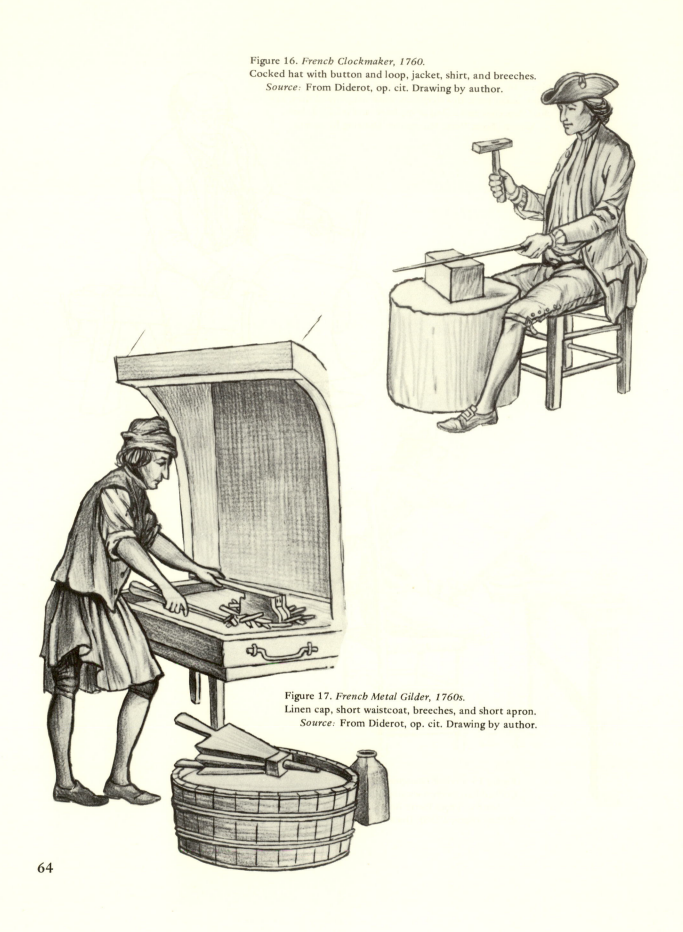

Figure 16. *French Clockmaker, 1760.*
Cocked hat with button and loop, jacket, shirt, and breeches.
Source: From Diderot, op. cit. Drawing by author.

Figure 17. *French Metal Gilder, 1760s.*
Linen cap, short waistcoat, breeches, and short apron.
Source: From Diderot, op. cit. Drawing by author.

64

Figure 18. *English Tanner, 1780s.*
Above his waistcoat is a sheepskin apron with an apron of leather over it. The leather leg guards are a protection from a powerful tanning fluid called "ooze" and from vitriolic acid, used in tanning the hides.
   Source: Copeland, op. cit.

Figure 19. *French Sheet Glass Worker, 1760s.*
A large leather apron covers his body from the throat to below the knees as a protection against the intense heat of the glass furnace. Beneath his apron he is dressed in shirt and breeches.
   Source: From Diderot, op. cit. Drawing by author.

Figure 20. *French Glass Blower, 1760s.*
The eye shield is a protection against the furnace heat. He also has on a linen cap, a loose smock, and a linen apron hanging from his neck down to his knees. He wears shoes, but no breeches or stockings.
   Source: From Diderot, op. cit. Drawing by author.

65

Figure 21. *Group of Foundry Workers, 1772-1775.*
Three of the men wear short jackets; the man on the left has
on a double-breasted jacket, and the man in the center, a sleeveless waistcoat. Two men wear cocked hats and the man on the
right has on a hat cocked up in the back. The seated man appears
to be wearing a wig and a ruffled shirt.
   Source: From watercolors done in the Royal Brass Foundry
at Woolwich, England, 1772-1775; Melvin H. Jackson and
Charles De Beer, *Eighteenth Century Gunfoundery* (Washington,
D.C., 1974). Drawing by author.

66

Figure 21A. *Tending a Furnace.*
The man on the right wears a smock, breeches, and leggings, and the other, a round hat with ribbon cockade, single-breasted coat, and apron.
 Source: From watercolors, Royal Brass Foundry; Jackson and De Beer, op. cit. Drawing by author.

Figure 21B. *Removing a Spindle from a Gun Mold.*
Both workers wear aprons, round hats, and breeches. The man on the left wears a short vest, and the other a skirted vest which was more common at the time.
 Source: From watercolors, Royal Brass Foundry; Jackson and De Beer, op. cit. Drawing by author.

67

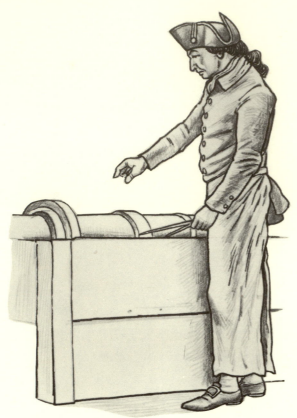

Figure 21C. *Positioning a Dolphin on a Howitzer.*
Cocked hat with button and loop, short jacket, and apron.
 Source: From watercolors, Royal Brass Foundry; Jackson and De Beer, op. cit. Drawing by author.

Figure 21D. *Two Styles of Working Dress.*
The two men on the right wear smocks and breeches; the man on the left, a shirt, waistcoat, breeches, and apron.
 Source: From watercolors, Royal Brass Foundry; Jackson and De Beer, op. cit. Drawing by author.

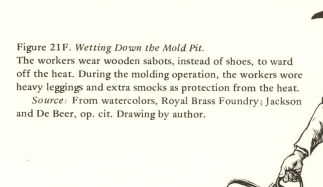

Figure 21F. *Wetting Down the Mold Pit.*
The workers wear wooden sabots, instead of shoes, to ward
off the heat. During the molding operation, the workers wore
heavy leggings and extra smocks as protection from the heat.
   Source: From watercolors, Royal Brass Foundry; Jackson
and De Beer, op. cit. Drawing by author.

Figure 21E. *Two Foundry Workmen.*
Both wear waistcoats, with and without sleeves and with short
and longer skirts. Both men wear neckerchiefs.
   Source: From watercolors, Royal Brass Foundry; Jackson
and De Beer, op. cit. Drawing by author.

69

Figure 22. *French Iron Foundry Worker.*
With the exception of his sabots, this French worker's dress
does not differ from that of the English. His bibbed apron,
probably of leather, was worn against the intense heat of the
furnace.
    Source: From Diderot, op. cit. Drawing by author.

Figure 23. *Belgian Coal Miners, 1770s.*
Their working dress consists of round felt hats, short waistcoats
without skirts, sleeved and sleeveless waistcoats, breeches,
heavy stockings, and shoes. Their leather harnesses with hooks
attached enable them to drag the coal carts through the mine
shafts.
    Source: From Leonard DeFrance, *The Colliery* (Musée de
l'Art Wallon, Liege, Belgium, 1778). Drawing by author.

70

Figure 24. *German Potter, 1774.*
He turns his potter's wheel with bare feet, and wears a cap,
probably of linen, a waistcoat, breeches, and a bibbed apron.
 Source: From Daniel Chodowieckis and J. B. Basedow,
Elementarerk (Berlin, 1774). Drawing by author.

Figure 25. *English Miller, Circa 1805.*
Cap, short sleeveless waistcoat without skirts, breeches, stockings, short leggings or half gaiters, and short apron tied at the
waist.
 Source: From Pyne, *Microcosm.* Drawing by author.

71

Figure 26. *English Slaughterhouse Worker, 1808.*
He has on a cap (probably knitted), a sleeveless waistcoat, and
two aprons. The upper apron, made of hide with the hair side
out, is bibbed and fastens to a waistcoat button on the breast.
The under apron might be of coarse linen, canvas, or leather.
On his legs he wears leather leggings that tie at the back.
   Source: From Pyne, *Microcosm.* Drawing by author.

Figure 27. *American Dyer, Late Eighteenth or Early
Nineteenth Century.*
Body shirt, apron, ribbed stockings, and slippers or mules
instead of shoes.
   Source: From *American Heritage History of Colonial
Antiques* (New York, 1967). Drawing by author.

72

Figure 28. *English Tailor, 1770s.*
This fashionable tailor wears his hair curled and powdered and has on a striped kerchief knotted about his throat. He carries a round hat cocked up like that of a seaman. His coat and waistcoat are single-breasted. He carries measuring tapes about his neck and his scissors in his waistcoat pocket. His shoes are light, fashionable, buckled pumps.
    Source: Copeland, op. cit.

Figure 29. *French Button Makers, 1760s.*
They are dressed in the typical working class style of the time.
    Source: An English copy of a Diderot plate by J. Lodge, undated, in the author's collection.

Figure 30. *English Hatter, 1750.*
His dress consists simply of cap, shirt, breeches, stockings, and shoes. In his hand he carries a hatting frame.

    Source: From a print in *Universal* magazine (London, April 1750). Drawing by author.

Figure 31. *German Carder of Wool, 1804.*
Cap, sleeveless waistcoat, shirt, breeches, stockings, slippers, and bibbed apron.

    Source: From a print in *Universal* magazine (London, April 1750). Drawing by author.

74

Figure 32. *Colonial Barber, Circa 1755.*
He wears a cocked hat with button and loop, and a single-breasted frock coat with vertical pockets. His bibbed white linen apron is buttoned to his waistcoat and tied at the waist. He wears breeches and fine silk stockings with clocks at the side. He carries a gentleman's wig, a shaving basin, and a device for powdering wigs. The barber himself wears a short bob wig with a comb stuck in it.
    Source: Copeland, op. cit.

Figure 33. *English Stocking Maker, Circa 1805.*
Single-breasted coat, apron, breeches, shoes, and stockings.
    Source: From *The Book of Trades* (New York, 1808), Vol. 3. Drawing by author.

75

Figure 34. *Rope Makers at Work, 1755.*
They all wear aprons and short jackets (the man on the far
right has embroidered buttonholes). Two men have on round
hats and the worker in the background, what appears to be a
fur cap.

    Source: An unidentified German print of 1775 in the
author's collection.

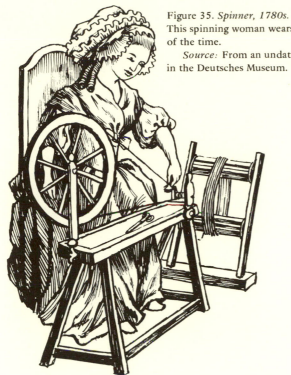

Figure 35. *Spinner, 1780s.*
This spinning woman wears the typical attire of a housewife of the time.
    Source: From an undated print entitled "Der Bortenwurker" in the Deutsches Museum. Drawing by author.

Figure 36. *English Milliner, 1771.*
She wears a flowered hat cocked rakishly over her eyes. Her hair is done in ringlets, and her decorative apron is short. For warmth she is wrapped in a dark shawl.
    Source: From a print entitled "The Charming Milliner of. . . . St.," by J. Smith and Robert Sayer, London, 1771. Drawing by author.

NOTES

1. Clarence Ver Steeg, *The Formative Years, 1607-1763* (New York, 1964), p. 247.
2. Ibid., p. 187.
3. Courtesy of George Shumway, Liberty Cap Books, York, Pennsylvania.

(4)
Tradesmen and Peddlers

The small merchants of colonial America were generally better off than those of Europe. The exception occurred during the depression of the 1760s when many were forced out of business and back into the ranks of the working class, while others barely managed to subsist by accepting payment in the form of farm produce or service.

INNKEEPERS

The colonial innkeeper occupied a different position in society than did his counterpart in old Europe. As many French visitors to eighteenth-century America observed, American innkeepers belonged to a higher social class than the European, many of them being retired army officers or persons of equally high rank.[1] An English observer shortly after the American Revolution reflected on the American innkeeper's higher status: "They will not bear the treatment we too often give ours at home. They feel themselves in some degree independent of travellers, as all of them have other occupations to follow; nor will they put themselves into a bustle on your account; but with good language, they are very civil, and will accommodate you as well as they can." Another French visitor noted the greater respectability of American inns: "You will not go into one without meeting neatness, decency, and dignity. The table is served by a maiden well-dressed and pretty; by a pleasant mother whose age has not effaced the agreeableness of her features; and by men who have that air of respectability which is inspired by the idea of equality, and are not ignoble and base like the greater part of our own tavern-keepers."[2]

The innkeeper's dress differed very little from that of the mercantile class. Like the small shopkeeper, he too usually wore an apron.

CHIMNEY SWEEPS

Because of the nature of his work, the chimney sweep usually had a small, wiry build. He was generally

Figure 1. *German Innkeeper, 1777.*
Knitted cap, short coatee or jacket, short bibbed apron, and breeches.
    Source: From an unidentified print at the Goethe Museum, Dusseldorf. Drawing by author.

assisted by a small boy, though it was not unknown for small girls to accompany him. The child's role was to climb up the chimney and remove the soot with scraper and broom; the sweep would then gather the soot at the bottom of the chimney. The sweep's standard attire was a jacket with belt, breeches, and cap—all of them constantly blackened, begrimed, and worn.

STREET VENDORS

Street vendors selling foods and household necessities were a common sight throughout the cities of the eastern seaboard in the 1700s. While some large markets offered fruits, fish, and meats, there were too few of them to service the needs of the total population. Hence, the street vendors became a staple on the colonial scene. Some vendors conducted their business at the same street corner for years; others wandered from street to street crying their wares.

Included in their ranks were oyster men, gingerbread ladies, pie men, hot corn girls, hominy sellers, honeycomb sellers, chicken and fish vendors, cheese men, peanut girls, muffin boys, sweet potato men, and brick dust sellers. Other commodities hawked in the streets included flowers, oranges, lavender, buttons, dumplings, rosemary and sweetbriar, old cloaks and coats, rabbits, mousetraps, brooms, and shoes.[3]

At the lower end of the scale of poverty among the street peddlers were the singers and sellers of ballads; they were virtually beggars. This group was composed mainly of women, many of whom were blind or crippled. While theirs was not an exceedingly profitable occupation, a real demand for their wares existed, for broadsheets of ballads were very popular in colonial America. Two of the most celebrated songs of the century were "Our Polly's a Sad Slut" and "Chevy Chase," the latter hailing the bravery of New England's soldiers during the capture of Louisbourg. In 1750, broadsheets normally sold for two pence in the streets of New York.

As for what the street vendor wore, we must rely on European sources. A number of interesting water-

80

Figure 2. *English Innkeeper, 1790.*
Close-bodied linen coat and an apron tied at the waist.
   Source: From *Catchpenny Prints,* by Bowles and Carver,
1750 to 1775 (London, 1970). Drawing by author.

colors by Nicolino Calyo are available for New York
City vendors. Unfortunately, however, they date from
1840 only.

BUTCHERS

The eighteenth-century butcher had a distinctive
working dress. From his belt hung a wooden case for
his knives and his ever-present sharpening steel. He
usually wore a cap and a red and white striped waistcoat. Sleeves covered the arm from the wrist to above
the elbow in order to protect the coat or shirt sleeves.
In the last years of the century, the butchers began to
adorn their blue aprons; this adornment was to become
the symbol of the profession during the nineteenth
century.

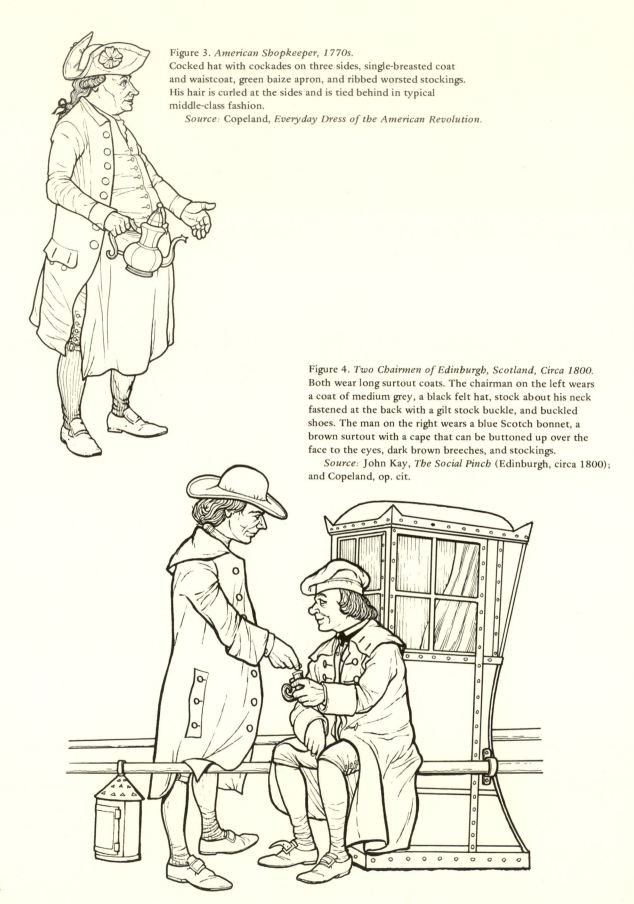

Figure 3. *American Shopkeeper, 1770s.*
Cocked hat with cockades on three sides, single-breasted coat
and waistcoat, green baize apron, and ribbed worsted stockings.
His hair is curled at the sides and is tied behind in typical
middle-class fashion.
   Source: Copeland, *Everyday Dress of the American Revolution.*

Figure 4. *Two Chairmen of Edinburgh, Scotland, Circa 1800.*
Both wear long surtout coats. The chairman on the left wears
a coat of medium grey, a black felt hat, stock about his neck
fastened at the back with a gilt stock buckle, and buckled
shoes. The man on the right wears a blue Scotch bonnet, a
brown surtout with a cape that can be buttoned up over the
face to the eyes, dark brown breeches, and stockings.
   Source: John Kay, *The Social Pinch* (Edinburgh, circa 1800);
and Copeland, op. cit.

Figure 5. *French Lantern Seller, 1740s.*
Cocked hat, surtout or great coat with cape and standing collar, and leggings buttoned and gartered, like a soldiers. He carries his tin lanterns in his hands and in a canvas haversack slung over his shoulder.
    Source: Copeland, op. cit.

Figure 6. *Chimney Sweep and His Boy, 1779.*
Both wear jackets (the man's is belted) and carry drop cloths upon which they gather the soot. The man wears a grimy felt hat, with a scarf bound about his head, and leggings made from strips of blanket tied below the knee and ankle. The boy wears a cap and slippers rather than shoes. The man carries a telescoping broom for reaching up chimneys.
    Source: Copeland, op. cit.

Figure 7. *English Mender of Chairs, Circa 1802.*
She wears a spotted kerchief over her white blouse. Her gown
is green and her shoes have buckles. Over her back is slung a
bundle of rushes for caning chair seats and backs. She carries
her child in a checked apron tied up at her waist.

    Source: A print in the author's collection, entitled "Chairs
to Mend, Soho Square," published by Richard Phillips, St.
Paul's Church Yard, London, 1804.

84

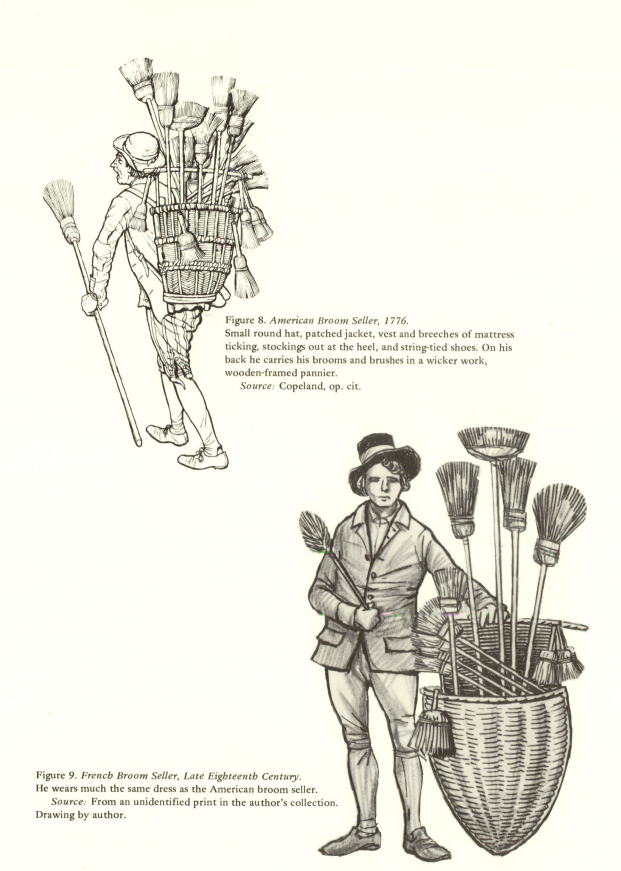

Figure 8. *American Broom Seller, 1776.*
Small round hat, patched jacket, vest and breeches of mattress ticking, stockings out at the heel, and string-tied shoes. On his back he carries his brooms and brushes in a wicker work, wooden-framed pannier.
    Source: Copeland, op. cit.

Figure 9. *French Broom Seller, Late Eighteenth Century.*
He wears much the same dress as the American broom seller.
    Source: From an unidentified print in the author's collection. Drawing by author.

Figure 10. *French Knife Sharpener from Auvergne, Circa 1730.*
An old hat cocked up, a bib apron which ties about the neck,
a single-breasted coat, and several pairs of stockings pulled over
one another, thrust into slippers.

   Source: From Edme Bouchardon, *Cris du Paris* (1735).
Drawing by author.

Figure 11. *American Knife Grinder, 1770s.*
He wears a battered round hat, a checked kerchief tied around
his neck, and single-breasted coat with a bibbed apron tied
over it. His leggings are made of mattress ticking and he wears
Indian-style moccasins. His grinding wheel is mounted on a
wooden frame with legs and is yoked about his neck with a
leather strap attached to the handles.

   Source: Copeland, op. cit.

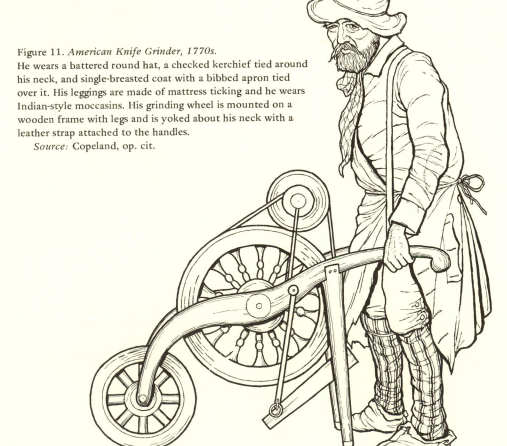

Figure 12. *American Water Carrier, 1770s.*
He wears an old cocked hat bound about his head with a
shawl, a coat cut in old-fashioned style, a spotted waistcoat,
and leather breeches. His carrying frame is supported by a
strap passing over his shoulders and attached to the handles
of his buckets.
    Source: Copeland, op. cit.

Figure 13. *Parisian Water Carrier, 1750.*
Cocked hat, single-breasted coat, and double-breasted waistcoat. His carrying frame is supported in the same manner as
above.
    Source: From *Ten Thousand Years of Daily Life*. Drawing
by author.

Figure 14. *English Gelder, Early Eighteenth Century.*
Round hat with ribbon cockade, single-breasted coat, apron,
shoes, and stockings.

 Source: From an undated print in the author's collection,
by I. Anderson, London. Drawing by author.

Figure 15. *English Street Peddler, 1750.*
His dress is indistinguishable from that of other working class
people of the streets.

 Source: George Paston, *Social Caricature in the 18th Century*
(London, 1905). Drawing by author.

Figure 16. *Oyster Vendor, 1790s.*
Small, round, battered hat, jacket, apron, breeches that tie
rather than buckle at the knee, and string-tied shoes.
   Source: From an unidentified print at the British Museum.
Drawing by author.

Figure 17. *Market Vendor, Paris, 1780s.*
The vendor is dressed, much like her costumer, in a linen mob
cap and striped gown. She wears an old belted coat with a
kerchief or shawl tied over it about her neck.
   Source: From *Ten Thousand Years of Daily Life.* Drawing
by author.

Figure 18. *Old Lady from Edinburgh, 1798.*
A hood that appears to be knitted, a short jacket, a gown that
reaches her ankles, several pairs of stockings, and string-tied
shoes. She supports her load by means of a head band.
    Source: A print in the author's collection, by John Kay,
Edinburgh, 1799.

90

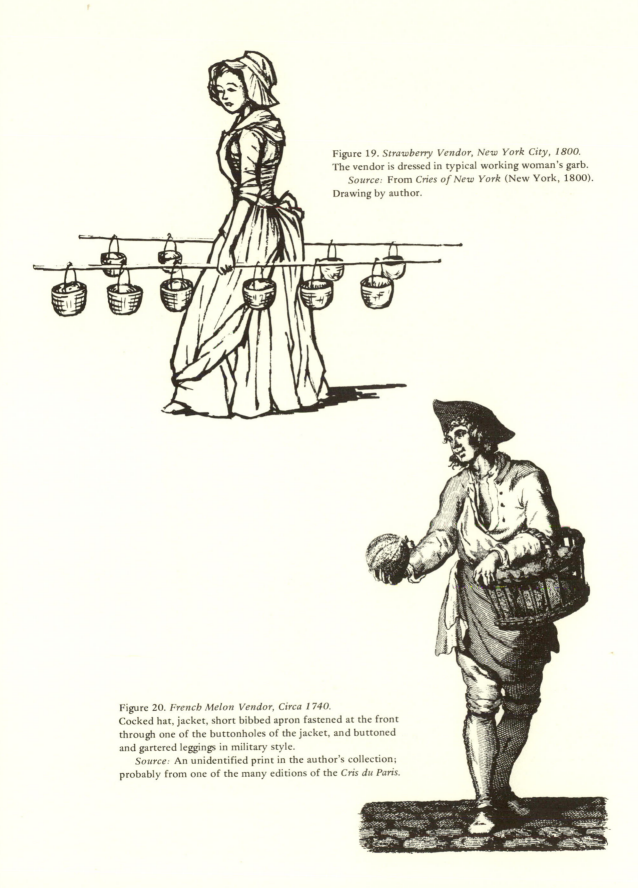

Figure 19. *Strawberry Vendor, New York City, 1800.*
The vendor is dressed in typical working woman's garb.
    Source: From *Cries of New York* (New York, 1800).
Drawing by author.

Figure 20. *French Melon Vendor, Circa 1740.*
Cocked hat, jacket, short bibbed apron fastened at the front
through one of the buttonholes of the jacket, and buttoned
and gartered leggings in military style.
    Source: An unidentified print in the author's collection;
probably from one of the many editions of the *Cris du Paris*.

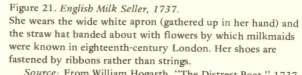

Figure 21. *English Milk Seller, 1737.*
She wears the wide white apron (gathered up in her hand) and
the straw hat banded about with flowers by which milkmaids
were known in eighteenth-century London. Her shoes are
fastened by ribbons rather than strings.
    Source: From William Hogarth, "The Distrest Poet," 1737.
Drawing by author.

Figure 22. *French Milk Seller, Circa 1755.*
She is bareheaded and wears a simple gown without the modest
benefit of a kerchief. She also wears an apron.
    Source: An unidentified print in the author's collection.

Figure 24. *Parisian Drink Vendor, Circa 1730.*
A cloth cap, coat cut double-breasted above the waist and
single-breasted below, somewhat like the coat worn by soldiers
of the time, apron, breeches, shoes, and stockings. His drink
container is hung knapsack style.
    Source: From Bouchardon, *Cris du Paris.* Drawing by author.

Figure 23. *Negro Buttermilk Seller, New York City,
Circa 1805-1808.*
Round hat that might be made of felt or straw, vest and shirt,
and striped trousers.
    Source: From *Cries of New York* (New York, 1800).
Drawing by author.

Figure 25. *Colonial Street Porter, Circa 1775.*
Cocked hat, single-breasted coat, vest, breeches, leggings, and "country boots" made of strips of blanket tied below the knee and at the ankle. On his back is a carrying frame, upon which he carries his burdens throughout the streets.
    Source: Copeland, op. cit.

Figure 26. *Italian Organ Grinder, 1720s.*
Single-breasted coat, ragged, cut-off breeches or trousers, shoes, and a cloak about his shoulders, which is probably nothing more than an old blanket.
    Source: From Filippo Bonanni, *Cabinetto Armonico* (Rome, 1723). Drawing by author.

94

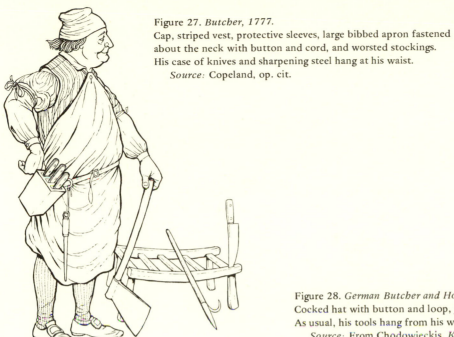

Figure 27. *Butcher, 1777.*
Cap, striped vest, protective sleeves, large bibbed apron fastened
about the neck with button and cord, and worsted stockings.
His case of knives and sharpening steel hang at his waist.
   Source: Copeland, op. cit.

Figure 28. *German Butcher and Housewife, 1770.*
Cocked hat with button and loop, jacket, apron, and neckcloth.
As usual, his tools hang from his waistbelt.
   Source: From Chodowieckis, *Künstlerfahrt nach danzig.*
Drawing by author.

95

Figure 29. *English Ballad Seller, Circa 1810.*
The ballad seller wears a man's felt hat adorned with a ribbon,
a hooded cloak, an apron, and one buckled shoe. On her right
foot she wears a worn out stocking.
Source: John Ashton, *Modern Street Ballads* (London, 1888).

NOTES

1. Sherrill, *French Memories of 18th Century America.*
2. Alice Morse Earle, *Stage-Coach and Tavern Days* (New York, 1969).
3. Esther Singleton, *Social New York Under the Georges, 1714-1776* (New York, 1902).

(5)
Frontiersmen and Pioneers

The great push to the interior, which culminated in the conquest of the West in the nineteenth century, had its origin in the eighteenth. The advance westward began from the eastern seaboard with the hunters, fur traders, and trappers. Next came the stockmen and farmers—most of them new migrants from Europe—who fenced in lands for cattle and sheep grazing, cleared the land for planting, and eventually established new towns. Throughout most of the century, the territorial goals of the pioneers were restricted to the Applachian mountain range. It was only after the Treaty of 1783 that they began to move toward the rich Mississippi River lands.[1]

Life for the frontiersmen and pioneers was rough and far cruder than the relatively settled existence known on the farms and in the towns of the seaboard colonies. Crucial to their ultimate taming of this new-found wilderness were their mechanical abilities and tools, particularly the ax and long rifle. Without some knowledge of Indian woodland crafts, they would not have adapted as successfully to frontier life. It was through the Indians that the frontiersmen first became acquainted with the canoe by which they were later able to navigate the rivers to reach new lands. From the Indians they had learned all the basics of survival in the wilderness: how to build shelter, prepare foods, and make clothing.[2]

FRONTIER DRESS

The dress of the more "civilized" East was of little use on the frontier. The dress that was worn in the West evolved from the conditions which the frontiersmen encountered, and, as such, it has been called the first uniquely American clothing.[3] At first, the clothing was made from the skins of wild animals, and here, again, the Indians were indispensable. The new settlers learned the Indians' method of curing and tanning and of making hunting smocks, leggings, and moccasins. Later, when the group seeking permanent homes arrived and brought spinning wheels and looms, linen and homespun replaced animal skins.[4]

Figure 1. *Typical Frontiersman, 1780s.*
Coonskin cap, fringed hunting shirt and leggings, Indian moc-
casins, leather belt with hunting knife, and long rifle.
Source: Drawing by author from various descriptions.

The basic outfit of the hunters, traders, and trappers of the mid-eighteenth century consisted of hunting shirt, leggings, cap, and moccasins. Their hunting shirts or smocks (also called "wamus") resembled loose tunics rather than coats. They were cut to just above the knees, had close-fitting sleeves and capes, and were open at the chest. While they were usually made of coarse linen (only rarely of tanned leather), sometimes homespun or linsey-woolsey was used. The bottom, front, cape, and sleeves were usually fringed.[5] In winter they would wear several body shirts under the hunting shirt and would wrap themselves, Indian-style, in a blanket or a Hudson's Bay blanket coat (or capote).

The fringed leggings reached from ankle to upper thigh and were secured to a leather waistbelt by thongs. They were made of leather and sometimes of fur. The waistbelt also supported a simple Indian breech clout, which could be drawn up between the legs and tucked through the back of the belt. At their side they often wore an Indian-style shot pouch, which was beaded and fringed. Near their right hand was a powder horn hanging from a leather thong or perhaps from a brightly beaded Indian belt. On the left side of the belt they carried a long hunting knife, secured in an Indian-style fringed and beaded sheath. On the right side they carried a tomahawk. The shot pouch might be decorated with strings of wampum beads in the Indian fashion.

Their headgear was sometimes no more than a kerchief bound about the head. The more usual custom, however, was a fur cap of coonskin, squirrel, fox, or bear with flaps attached for winter wear, or a round felt hat with a decorative band, perhaps made of rattlesnake skin.

An excellent description of frontier dress appears in an anonymous report of the Boone expedition, which took its westward journey from the banks of the Yadkin River in North Carolina on 25 September 1773:

At the head of the column marched a group of woodsmen, all of course, bearing rifles. Some strode on foot but many of them, perhaps the majority, were mounted on horses that walked slowly along.

98

Figure 2. *Pioneer Wife, Circa 1780.*
Round felt hat, kerchief, shawl, coarse linen apron, woolen stockings, and Indian moccasins.
   Source: Drawing by author from various descriptions.

They wore loose hunting shirts, and trousers of dressed deerskin, gayley decorated with the colored fringes so widely affected as a backwoods fashion. Their feet were clad in moccasins and on their heads were many sorts of fantastic caps of skins or of linsey woolsey, each fashioned according to the whim of its owner. Every man was girt with a leather belt from the right side of which hung a tomahawk to be used either as a hatchet or for some more violent purpose. On his left side he carried his hunting knife, a full powder horn, a leather pouch of home made bullets and another large leather pouch holding a quart or two of parched corn.

By 1817 Kentucky was not quite the frontier wilderness it had been forty-four years earlier, as is shown in the following: "The dress of the people is simple, the men wear a home manufactured cotton coat, or a hunting shirt, and a pair of trousers, with seldom any handkerchief around their neck. The men are fond of roving about in the woods with their rifle and dog."

Frontier women wore bodices made of fustian or linsey-woolsey or leather. Their chemises, made of coarse linen or cotton, were worn under the bodice. Their dresses had full skirts, though not as full or as long as those adopted by rural women in the more settled areas.[6] Whenever they wore a hat, it was usually a man's round felt hat. They were more likely, however, to wear a kerchief or knitted shawl over their heads. In winter they wrapped themselves in a blanket, Indian fashion, whenever they ventured outside. As for footgear, they went barefoot for most of the summer and wore Indian moccasins in the winter. Coarse linen aprons and, in winter, woolen stockings completed their costume.

The dress of Canadian frontiersmen (mostly French) and settlers differed somewhat from that of their cousins to the south. For one thing, the Canadian's dress was much more colorful. Another difference—their heavier clothing—was necessitated by the area's harder winters. A good description of the Canadian's winter dress was

Figure 3. *Backwoodsman and His Dog, 1810.*
This woodsman wears a round felt hat, tattered frock coat, leather breeches, and cloth gaiters over his shoes.
    Source: Adapted from a sketch by Joshua Shaw, circa 1810; Dunbar, *History of Travel in America,* Vol. 1. Drawing by author.

provided by a German officer stationed at Batiscan in November 1776:

> *He makes his own souliers des sauvages and also a piece of specially dressed leather. These are without heels, straps or ties, and when new do not look bad. We shall try the fashion this winter, for every one says we should freeze our feet in our boots or shoes. They tie their thick knitted brown stockings firmly under the knee with a red woolin band. Their breeches are of coarse cloth or home-dressed buffalo leather and their under shirt which laps over and is tied without any folds, they usually make of a homespun speckled woolen goods, such as many of our peasants make too. Their dress is trimmed at the hips with homemade thick woolen scarves with long tassels; these scarves are in all colors to suit one's fancy. On the back of the coat sits a capuchin cape of the same goods, which they all pull over their heads in stormy or wet weather. They rarely wear hats; the thick fulled caps, red outside and white inside, are the almost universal head covering. If the Canadian is fashionable he wears a jacket of a kind of white baize with blue or red ribbons in front and some rosettes of the same ribbon. The selvedge of the cloth is left along the bottom of the coat. This garment or jacket is national and is very comfortable fitting and warm.*[7]

The leggings they wore may have been similar to the Indians' or they may have been a form of country boot, "pieces of cloth folded around the leg and tied at the knee and ankle."[8]

    Unfortunately, contemporary illustrations of life on the American frontier during the eighteenth century are extremely rare. It is important to emphasize that many paintings and drawings done in the middle and late nineteenth century portray the early pioneers in fanciful regalia that have little to do with their actual appearance.

100

Figure 4. *Horse Barrow, 1810.*
The boy wears a round "bullycock" hat, short jacket, linen shirt, and leather breeches.
   Source: Adapted from a sketch by Joshua Shaw in Dunbar, op. cit. Drawing by author.

Figure 5. *Pioneer Woodcutters, 1810.*
These American woodcutters wear coarse linen shirts, leather breeches, and waistcoats without shirts, in the style of 1785-1815.
   Source: Adapted from a sketch by Joshua Shaw in Dunbar, op. cit., p. 282. Drawing by author.

Figure 6. *Traveler on a Flat Boat, 1810.*
This rustic traveler aboard a river craft wears a farmer's round hat and linen smock. A neckerchief is tied around his neck, and his breeches are of leather. On his feet he wears Indian moccasins.
    Source: Adapted from a sketch by Joshua Shaw in Dunbar, op. cit., p. 282. Drawing by author.

Figure 7. *Canadian on Snow Shoes, 1753.*
This French-Canadian trapper wears a round felt hat, single-breasted coat, breeches, and snowshoes adopted from the Indians. From his waist belt is suspended a belt axe and two pouches decorated with brass chains, common embellishments of the seventeenth century.
    Source: From *Histoire de l'Amerique Septentrionale* (Paris, 1722). Drawing by author.

Figure 8. *Canadian Farmer, 1778.*
"White capote trimmed with light blue ribbons and stripes. Red stock at the neck. Blue, red, yellow, and white striped sash around the waist. Buff breeches and brown and white striped leggings fastened by a garter below the knee."
    Source: From Albert Haarmann and Donald Holst, "The Friedrich von Germann Drawings of Troops in the American Revolution," *Military Collector and Historian* (Spring 1964). Drawing by author.

NOTES

1. Warwick, Pitz, and Wyckoff, *Early American Dress,* p. 271.
2. Ibid., p. 265.
3. Ibid., p. 271.
4. Ibid., p. 267.
5. Ibid., p. 268.
6. Ibid., p. 270.
7. John Palmer, *Journal of Travels in the United States of America and in Lower Canada Performed in the Year of 1817* (London: Sherwood, Neely, and Jones, 1818).
8. Thomas Anbury, *Travels Through the Interior Parts of America* (London, 1791).

(6)
Transportation
Workers

By 1763, the entire eastern seaboard, from
Maine to Georgia, was connected by a network of roads.
While these road systems were extremely primitive,
they represented a definite improvement over the foot-
paths and trails of the previous century. The better
roads were usually about eight feet wide, sometimes
cut with small ditches on either side to drain off rain
water. Most of them, however, made for arduous jour-
neys. One such road was typically so bad "as to greatly
delay the post riders and travelers in general. Trees
have fallen across it and are seldom removed. . . . A
number of the causeways are swamps and full of holes,
and many of the bridges are almost impassable."[1] In
an attempt to improve transportation, all of the colonies
passed road laws, some as early as the seventeenth century. But such efforts were to little avail, as it was difficult to enforce them.

For those who could afford it, the stage wagon was
the most popular method of travel. (Public stage coaches
were not introduced until the early nineteenth century.)
This vehicle traveled from one city to another in stages,
changing wagons several times along the way. In the
1760s, passengers could travel from New York City to
Philadelphia and back in five days for twenty shillings.
The fastest wagons, known as "Flying Machines," were
more expensive. Physically, the stage wagon was a long
car with three benches inside holding nine passengers.
On the front bench, with the driver, sat a tenth passenger. From the roof of the wagon hung three curtains,
all of which could be rolled up or lowered, depending
on the weather. As there was no baggage space, each
passenger had to fit his bags as best he could under his
legs or on his lap. The benches had no backs; hence,
a long journey over ill-made or bad roads was a fatigu-
ing affair indeed.

Wealthy urban people had their own private coaches,
with liveried coachmen and footmen. The southern
planters kept their coaches and six with slaves in attend-
ance. By 1776, the use of these coaches had become
widespread among the affluent in all the colonies. At
this time Philadelphia already had eighty-four private
coaches among her citizens.[2]

Figure 1. *Typical Coachman, 1780s.*
Below his great coat he wears a long, single-breasted, close-bodied coat and striped waistcoat without skirts. He carries a cocked hat and wears boots.
  Source: Copeland, *Everyday Dress of the American Revolution.*

As settlers moved westward and southward from the seaboard colonies, inland trade gradually followed. The Conestoga wagon, that uniquely American vehicle, evolved from the English country wagon and the great Dutch wagon in the early eighteenth century along the Conestoga River in Pennsylvania. By 1765, the wagon makers of Lancaster County had produced twenty thousand of these vehicles. The weight of the wagons and the huge Conestoga horses that drew them amazed foreign visitors.

It has been estimated that, by 1770, three thousand wagons a year, coming from as far as three hundred miles inland, delivered tobacco, flour, flaxseed, and other bulk loads to Charleston, South Carolina.[3] The most important and most heavily traveled road in all of the American colonies was the Philadelphia wagon road, which ran west out of Philadelphia to Lancaster, Pennsylvania, into the valley of Virginia, and on into the Piedmont area of North Carolina. This was the route taken by the Scotch-Irish and German immigrants traveling south.

The rough and ready waggoners of colonial America were intensely proud of their well-kept teams, despising comfort and indulging, most of them, in copious amounts of Monongohela whiskey. Many teamsters worked on their farms in the summer season and drove their wagons in winter; these were known as militia teamsters. A poem written in the mid-nineteenth century proclaimed the old-time waggoners to be superior to the militia teamsters:

> The "Regulars" were haughty men
> Since five or six they always drove
> With broad-tread wheels and English beds,
> They bore their proud and lofty heads,
> And always thought themselves above
> The homespun plain Militia men,
> Who wagoned only now and then. . .[4]

DRESS

The public coachman was an imposing figure. He

Figure 2. *American Waggoner, 1770s.*
His round felt hat is bound about the crown with a ribbon done in a cockade on the left side, in emulation of the soldiers of the time. He wears a waggoner's frock, a long smock-like shirt much like the rifle shirt or hunting shirt also worn by many soldiers. Around his legs he wears "country boots."
Source: Copeland, op. cit.

usually wore a caped, close-fitting great coat called a "wrap-rascal" that came to his knees, jackboots, and sometimes a gold laced hat. (The term *wrap-rascal* apparently derived from the fact that the great coat was closely modeled on the coat style worn by highway-men.)[5] In winter he added a fur cap, gloves, and scarlet sash.[6] When working on his horses at the stable, he wore a long, coarse linen smock like that of farmers and waggoners. These coachmen carried themselves with an uncommon arrogance. They were the envy of small boys as they sat high above the crowd, often the worse for brandy.[7]

An early American stage coachman is described as wearing calfskin boots, fur-lined overshoes, and home-spun garments below a great coat of fur. He wore a fur cap and a red sash with tassels about his waist. He also carried a blunderbuss in his box since colonial stage coaches had no guard.[8] Colonial waggoners wore long woolen hunting shirts with a large cape trimmed in red.[9]

Postillions (servants who rode on the near horse of one of the pairs attached to a coach or post chaise) to wealthy families wore livery like that of house servants. (For a further description of postillions, see Chapter 10.) Tobias Smollett describes the dress of a well-appointed English postillion: he was "a smart fellow, with a narrow-brimmed hat, with gold cording, a cut bob [wig], a decent blue jacket, leather breeches, and a clean linen shirt, puffed above the waistband."[10] In families of more modest means, such servants dressed less ostentatiously.

107

Figure 3. *English Waggoner Accosted by Highwayman, 1750.*
Waggoner's frock, round hat, and boots.

    Source: A print in the author's collection, by J. Atkins,
entitled "John Cottington alias Mol-Sack, Robbing the Oxford
Wagon," London, 1750.

Figure 4. *Two Teamsters of the Continental Army's Corps of Waggoners, 1779.*
One has a brown coat, green jacket, buckskin breeches, white yarn stockings, and felt hat. The other wears a nankeen coat, brown jacket, green breeches, blue ribbed stockings, old shoes, and beaver hat with a white button.
   Source: From *Pennsylvania Packet,* 20 March 1779. Drawing by author.

Figure 5. *German Postillion, 1790s.*
Round black hat, pale buff jacket, leather breeches, and heavy
postillion's boots and spurs. He carries a whip and wears a
coiled post horn on a cord over his shoulder.
Source: From "Posting in Germany," by Thomas Rowlandson,
1790s. Drawing by author.

Figure 6. *Water Cart Driver, New York City, Circa 1805.*
Small round hat, body shirt, coarse smock of unbleached linen,
leather breeches, thread stockings, and buckled shoes.
    Source: From an undated watercolor on cardboard drawing
by Walter Chappel, Edward C. Arnold collection, Metropolitan
Museum of Art, New York. Drawing by author.

NOTES

1. Oscar T. Barck and Hugh T. Lefler, *Colonial America* (New York, 1958).
2. Ibid.
3. Bridenbaugh, *Cities in Revolt.*
4. "Waggoning," by H. L. Fisher (New York, 1929).
5. Warwick, Pitz, and Wyckoff, *Early American Dress,* p. 159.
6. Earle, *Two Centuries of Costume in America* pp. 622-623.
7. Cunnington, Lucas, and Mansfield, *Occupational Costume in England;* Rosamond Bayne-Powell, *Travelers in 18th Century England* (London, 1951).
8. Earle, *State-Coach and Tavern Days,* pp. 323-325.
9. George Shumway, *Conestoga Wagon, 1750-1850* (York, Pennsylvania, 1966).
10. Tobias Smollett, *Humphry Clinker* (London, 1771).

(7)
Public Servants

By the beginning of the American Revolution, most colonial towns had some kind of fire, policing, street cleaning, sanitation, and street lighting provisions. Generally, the colonists were more successful than the Europeans in solving the problems of public service. Despite these better efforts, however, they shared the same fire and public safety hazards throughout the century.

Boston was the first American city to establish a regular fire department with hand engines and fire buckets. The Boston Fire Society was established in 1717, and by 1743 Boston had eight fire companies in operation. Philadelphia organized its Union Fire Company in 1736.[1]

By 1750, several American cities had in their employ a "scavenger raker, or other officer" to clean the streets, lanes, and alleys. The scavenger raker carried away "ashes, dirt, filth, and soyle" which had been thrown into the streets.[2] In 1755, William Livingston of New York City mentioned the unpleasant effect that was produced by "the putrid stench arising from that sink of corruption," Rotten Row, and he demanded that this open sewer be filled.[3] As early as 1744, New York City had passed a street cleaning law requiring all citizens to clean up the filth in front of their houses and kennels. In 1750, Philadelphia's Mayor Thomas Laurence accused the citizens of heaping great piles of dirt and filth in the gutters, thereby creating "an intolerable stench. . . whereby distempers will in all probability be occasioned."[4] Even so, American cities were much cleaner than the cities of Europe.

Other sanitation workers included the night soil carters, employed both in the colonies and Europe. The carters would make their rounds in the small hours of the morning, collecting the contents of chamber pots which they then dumped into the night cart.

The eighteenth-century city did not have an organized police force as we know it today; rather, a system of evening security which dated back to the Middle Ages—the "night watch"—was in use. The colonial watchman had far-ranging duties: he was expected to keep an eye out

Figure 1. *English Fireman, 1785-1790.*
Helmet, short working man's jacket, breeches, and heavy leather boots similar to those worn by fishermen of the time. His helmet resembles that prescribed and worn by pioneers and artificers of the British Army in the 1750s.
    Source: From *The Watercolor Drawings of Thomas Rowlandson,* from the Wiggen collection, Boston Public Library (New York, 1947). Drawing by author.

for horse thieves, burglars, hostile Indians (in frontier towns), and runaway slaves. His equipment usually consisted of a heavy staff and lantern. In addition, some watchmen were armed with a musket or pike. In England, the night watchmen carried so-called battle rattles, wooden devices which, when spun vigorously, gave off a sharp machinegun-like clatter in order to summon assistance and raise an alarm in emergencies.

The watchman walked his weary rounds in the towns of colonial America, calling out the time and the weather each hour. With his long staff and horn lantern, he was hardly a formidable figure. The watchman of the towns of Nazareth and Bethlehem, Pennsylvania, would cry out a pious liturgy:

> *Four o'clock*
> *The hour is four! Where-ere on earth are three*
> *The Lord has promised he the fourth shall be.*[5]

The French visitor in the late eighteenth century, Moreau de St. Méry, described the pleasure he would experience in laying snug in his warm bed during the early hours of a frosty morning and hearing the watchman's call that it was snowing outside.[6]

Another duty of the watchman was to check that all shop and house doors were locked and to warn the proprietors if he found any were insecure. By 1770, Philadelphia had a paid watch, with orders to apprehend "all night walkers, malefactors, rogues, vagabonds, and disorderly persons, whom they shall find to be disturbing the peace." Philadelphia's night watch cost the city five hundred pounds a year in the 1740s.[7]

Watchmen in New York City in 1773 were provided with "centinel boxes" and uniforms, including bearskin caps for the two captains of the watch. Night watchmen in the larger cities were superintended by constables. The constable's job was not an easy one. One constable in Philadelphia came to grief on an evening in the 1760s when he tried to break up a fight near a house of prostitution. He was beaten to death by several sailors, and several members of his watch were also mauled.[8]

114

Figure 2. *English Fireman, "British Crown Fire Office," 1735.*
Single-breasted jacket, breeches, and helmet (probably of leather).
A written description of a fireman's dress from 1750 mentions
a coat with buttons to the waist, a single-breasted waistcoat,
breeches, a leather helmet with crest, wide brim and neck flap
at the back, leather shoes with large buckles, and a badge on
the arm of the coat.
    Source: From Cunnington, Lucas, and Mansfield, *Occupational
Costume in England.* Drawing by author.

Although most of the larger American cities had a
hired-and-paid night watch, some of them had a "citizen's watch" made up of citizen volunteers. Generally,
members of the citizen's watch were not highly regarded.
In one description they are reviled as "a parcel of idle,
drinking, vigilant snorers, who never quelled any noc-
turnal tumult in their lives [nor, as far as we can learn,
were ever able to discover a fire breaking out], but
would perhaps, be as ready to join in a burglary as any
thief in Christiandom."[9] The city of New York, perhaps
alert to the failings of the volunteer system and spurred
on by a mythical slave uprising, the so-called Negro
Conspiracy of 1741, established a paid watch system
before 1745.

Another colonial public servant was the lamplighter
who was employed to trim and clean the street lamps
in the afternoon and to light the lamps at dark. At mid-
night he would renew the fuel in those lamps needing
it. The lamplighters had no distinctive clothing, but
with their ladders and pots containing fuel oil for the
lamps, they were easily identified on the streets of an
eighteenth-century town.

After Philadelphia installed whale oil street lamps
in 1751, the city became known as the one with the
best lighting in all the British empire. By 1752 private
citizens installed new glass lamps in New York City,
while many shopkeepers placed "globe" street lamps
in front of their shops. The Bostonians financed their
street lamps in 1773 by means of a public tax.[10]

The individual American colonies established their
own independent postal systems, the Dutch at New
Netherlands being among the first in 1652. Virginia
also set up a regular postal system early—in 1662. In
1711, Parliament included the colonial post offices as
part of the imperial postal system. Later, in 1753,
Benjamin Franklin, then Postmaster General of the
colonies, together with Assistant Postmaster William
Hunter, so improved the colonial postal system that
in two short years post riders were delivering the mail
every week, all year round, from Philadelphia to New
England. At the onset of the Revolution, the colonists

Figure 3. *London Dustman, 1750.*
Round hat, long belted jacket, breeches, and short gaiters. At his belt is a bag or purse, probably made of canvas or coarse linen, for the accumulated street rubbish.
Source: From M. Dorothy George, *Hogarth to Cruikshank, Social Change in Graphic Satire* (New York, 1967), p. 49. Drawing by author.

established the Constitutional Post by Subscription and were strongly supported in this effort by patriotic groups such as the Sons of Liberty. Throughout the century the life of the colonial post rider was neither easy nor comfortable. Exposed in all seasons to wind and weather, he also had to contend with tired horses, occasional robbers, hostile Indians, and roads that were often little better than trails.

DRESS

In England in the 1770s, the post boy often drove a mail coach or a small carriage, the post chaise, which could carry two passengers. By this time he was generally uniformed and was sometimes accompanied by an armed guard uniformed in green or, more likely, red with gold binding.

Figure 4. *English Carters, 1780s.*
They are dressed as ordinary working men with nothing in
their dress distinguishing their occupation.
    Source: From *Catchpenny Prints*, by Bowles and Carver.
Drawing by author.

Figure 5. *Typical Watchman.*
Round hat, surtout coat, and belted jacket. He wears a rattle
on a cord and carries a large tin lantern and staff.
    Source: Copeland, *Everyday Dress of the American
Revolution.*

Figure 6. *London Watchman, 1779.*
He wields his rattle to summon assistance.
    Source: From a print entitled "The Anatomist Overtaken
by the Watch in Carrying off Miss W___tts in a Hamper,"
by W. Austin, 1779. Drawing by author.

Figure 7. *Night Watchman, New York City, Circa 1750.*
He is dressed identically to the London watchmen.
 Source: From an unidentified print in *Album of American History, Colonial Period* (New York, 1944), p. 255. Drawing by author.

Figure 8. *Typical London Lamplighter, 1780s.*
His double-breasted jacket is made of mattress ticking, beneath which he wears a double-breasted vest with an edged binding. He carries a cluster of lamp wicks in a rope belt, with scissors for trimming the wicks. He also wears a short apron and striped stockings.
 Source: Copeland, op. cit.

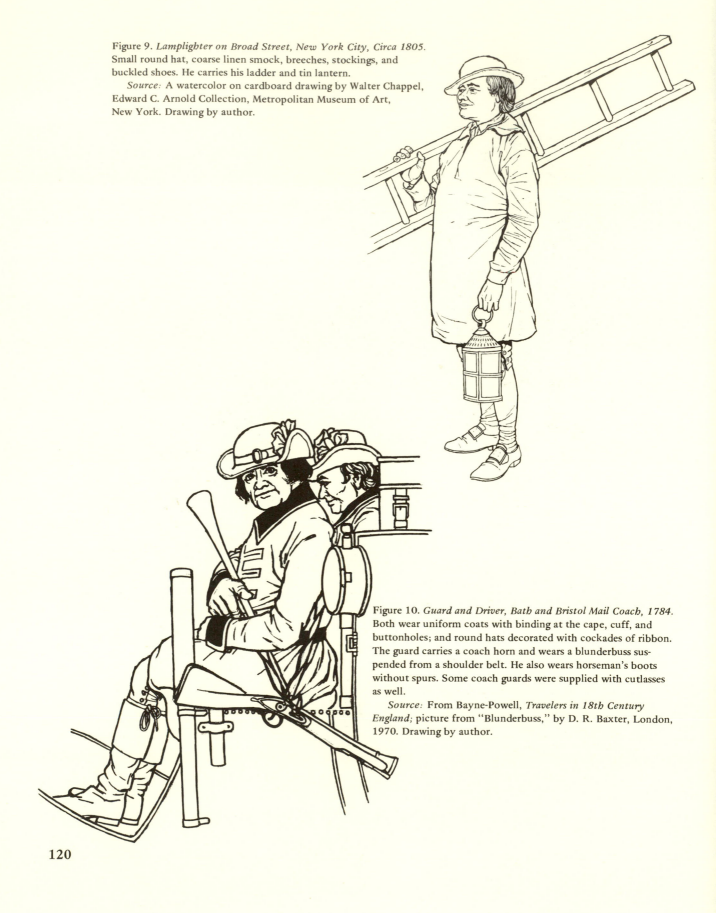

Figure 9. *Lamplighter on Broad Street, New York City, Circa 1805.*
Small round hat, coarse linen smock, breeches, stockings, and
buckled shoes. He carries his ladder and tin lantern.
   Source: A watercolor on cardboard drawing by Walter Chappel,
Edward C. Arnold Collection, Metropolitan Museum of Art,
New York. Drawing by author.

Figure 10. *Guard and Driver, Bath and Bristol Mail Coach, 1784.*
Both wear uniform coats with binding at the cape, cuff, and
buttonholes; and round hats decorated with cockades of ribbon.
The guard carries a coach horn and wears a blunderbuss suspended from a shoulder belt. He also wears horseman's boots
without spurs. Some coach guards were supplied with cutlasses
as well.
   Source: From Bayne-Powell, *Travelers in 18th Century
England;* picture from "Blunderbuss," by D. R. Baxter, London,
1970. Drawing by author.

Figure 11. *American Post Rider, 1775.*
Leather helmet ("a well-guarded leather cap" was prescribed
for post boys in England), coat, gauntlets, and boots. He appears
about to sound his post horn (identical to a coach horn) as he
gallops toward town. Behind the saddle is the mail valise.

Source: From a device used in the Masthead of the newspaper *Boston Post Boy* (circa 1750). Drawing by author.

Figure 12. *Colonial Post Rider, 1770s.*
Leather cap similar to a dragoon's cap, with a cloth turban
tied about the crown; great coat, probably red, though he
might be wearing a Roquelaure. This garment ("Roccelo,"
"Rocklo," "Rocket," "Roquelo," as it was variously called)
was a cloak that came to the knees and buttoned down the
front, with a large single or double collar split in the back for
wearing on horseback.

Source: Cunnington and Lucas, *Occupational Costume in
England.* Drawing by author.

121

Figure 13. *Female Sexton, Mid-eighteenth Century England.*
The lady shown here is obviously equipped for grave digging.
She wears a man's round hat and a buff waistcoat. A green
kerchief is knotted about her neck and she wears what would
appear to be a man's single-breasted snuff-colored coat. Her
gown is also a snuff-colored brown.

   Source: An undated anonymous print in the author's
collection.

I KAY 1809

BEETTY DICK TOWN CRIER IN DALKEITH
BORN 1693 DIED 1773

291

NOTES

1. Barck and Lefler, *Colonial America.*
2. Ibid.
3. Ibid.
4. Ibid.
5. Earle, *Stage-coach and Tavern Days.*
6. *Travels in America,* by Moreau de Saint Méry, 1792-93
   (New York, 1953).
7. Bridenbaugh, *Cities in Revolt.*
8. Ibid.
9. Esther Singleton, *Social New York Under the Georges,*
   1714-1776 (New York, 1902).
10. Ibid.

Figure 14. *Town Crier, Dalkeith, Scotland, 1809.*
White linen hood, blue-grey jacket, and light brown skirt. Her
shoes are fastened with strings rather than buckles.
   Source: A print in the author's collection, by John Kay,
Edinburgh, 1809.

123

(8)
Soldiers and Militia Men

Prior to the Revolution, the colonists had served in both regular British regiments and colonial and militia units. They had had considerable military experience, having participated in the many wars and campaigns of the eighteenth century against the French, Spanish, and Indians. Each colony had a militia system and could put men in the field, though the expense of outfitting militia and colonial regiments was unpopular with the citizenry. The militia men usually had no uniforms and were ill-equipped. Most militia acts stipulated merely that a soldier should receive a musket, a bayonet or cutting hatchet, a cartridge box with cartridges, and a blanket. The arms which the colonial government issued, however, were often poor, and recruits were encouraged to bring their own weapons. The Commonwealth of Pennsylvania allowed a recruit a half dollar if he supplied his own gun and blanket. In many cases the soldiers were expected to provide their own uniforms as well. For example, orders issued in 1755 at Fort Cumberland, Maryland, for the outfitting of the officer corps of the Virginia Regiment stated that every officer was "to provide himself with a suit of regimentals of good blue cloth; the coat to be faced and cuffed with scarlet, and trimmed with silver; a scarlet waistcoat with silver lace; blue breeches, and a silver-laced hat, if to be had, for garrison duty."[1]

The Pennsylvania Regiment, consisting chiefly of frontiersmen along the Susquehanna River in 1755, was a typical regiment of the times. In 1757 it was decided that the regiment should be clothed in green coats, red waistcoats, and leather breeches—at their own expense. Not surprisingly, for the first two years the soldiers had no uniforms. It was then suggested that the regiment purchase seamen-style dress: "Petticoat trousers reaching to the thick of the leg, made of strong linen, and a sailor's frock made of the same." Most of the men ended up wearing their own clothing. Newspaper descriptions of deserters mention blue stockings, light-colored coats, and white linen caps among other items. Many of the men wore hunting shirts of coarse linen, Indian leggings, and moccasins.

Figure 1. *Member of the South Carolina Regiment of Horse, 1740-1749.*
Mazarine blue broadcloth coats with brass buttons, red waistcoats, buckskin breeches, and gold laced hats.
Source: Courtesy of the Company of Military Historians Magazine, MUIA plates 389-390, by Peter Copeland and Fitzhugh McMaster.

A number of colonial military units of the 1750s wore Indian dress, among them the Virginians that Colonel George Washington marched up to Raystown, Pennsylvania. The English soldiers who were stationed in the colonies also adopted some articles of Indian dress, notably Indian leggings, moccasins, and hunting shirts.[2] Later, during the war for independence, Washington ordered Indian boots or leggings for his soldiers instead of stockings.[3]

At the outset of the Revolutionary War, many of the newly raised units, especially those from rural and back country areas, were composed of riflemen. These rifle units usually adopted a distinctive dress: fringed hunting (or rifle) shirts made of coarse linen dyed green, black, brown, blue, or yellow, capes and shirt cuffs of a distinctive color, overalls or thin, fringed, linen trousers, flopped hat, shot bag, and powder horn.[4] Patrick Henry's riflemen wore shirts and breeches made of tow cloth.[5] The rifle shirts were made of any material available and differed according to the origin of the regiment. Colonel Henry Babcock's Rhode Island State Regiment wore rifle dress dyed purple or "claret colored."[6] A soldier of the 7th Virginia Regiment was described in May 1776 to be wearing "a striped Virginia cloth hunting shirt dyed almost black."[7] One of the best descriptions of the uniquely American rifle dress, as worn by the famous Daniel Morgan's Rifle Company, comes to us from John Trumbull in 1775:

> *You expressed apprehension that the rifle dress of General Morgan may be mistaken hereafter for a waggoner's frock, which he, perhaps, wore when on the expedition with General Braddock; there is no more resemblance between the two dresses, than between a cloak and a coat; the waggoner's frock was intended, as the present cartman's, to cover and protect their other clothes, and is merely a long coarse shirt reaching below the knee; the dress of the Virginia rifle-men who came to Cambridge in 1775 [among whom was Morgan] was an elegant loose dress reach-*

ing to the middle of the thigh, ornamented with fringes in various parts and meeting the pantaloons of the same material and color, fringed and ornamented in a corresponding style. The officers wore the usual crimson sash over this, and around the waist, the straps, belts, etc. were black, forming, in my opinion, a very picturesque and elegant as well as useful dress. It cost a trifle; the soldier could wash it at any brook he passed; however worn and ragged and dirty his other clothing might be, when this was thrown over it, he was in elegant uniform.

The above is the outfit that Morgan is shown wearing in Trumbull's painting of Burgoyne's surrender at Saratoga. The attire of the average soldier of the Revolution, however, was probably closer to the waggoner's frock mentioned in this description than to the elegant dress of the Virginia riflemen.

Later in the war, in 1779, the Board of War specified exact uniforms, both in color and cut, for the regiments of the Continental Army. At last, it seemed, the Army would receive regulation uniforms, as did the armies of the European nations. In the General Order of 2 October 1779, Washington spelled out what these uniforms would be:

Artillery and artillery artificer regiments would wear a dark blue coat faced and lined with scarlet with yellow buttons, the buttonholes to be bound with yellow tape. The light dragoons would wear dark blue coats faced with white and white buttons. The infantry regiments would wear dark blue coats lined with white, and white buttons; the facings of the coats were to be as follows:

New Hampshire, Massachusetts, Rhode Island and Connecticut soldiers to wear white facings.

New York and New Jersey troops were to wear buff facings.

Pennsylvania, Delaware, Maryland and

Figure 2. *Virginia "Shirtmen," 1776.*
The figures depicted here are in the typical rifleman's dress adopted by many American units at the outset of the war. The second figure from the left, an officer, wears a purple shirt and trousers with white fringes. The men wear brownish-green outfits with "Liberty or Death" emblazoned across the front and felt hats, uncocked, with buck's tails fastened in them.
  Source: Courtesy of the Company of Military Historians, MUIA plate "The Minute Battalion of Culpepper County, Virginia, 1775-1776," by Peter Copeland and Marko Zlatich.

Figure 3. *Member of a "Silk Stocking Company," New York City.*
The Sportsmen Company was composed of well-to-do young
men of the city who in 1775 formed Colonel John Lasher's
battalion of New York State troops. Their uniforms are described as consisting of "green short coats faced with crimson,
and small round hats."
 Source: E. C. O'Callaghan, *Documents Relative to the
Colonial History of New York* (1898) Vol. 1.

Virginia troops were to wear red facings.
 *North Carolina, South Carolina and Georgia
troops were to wear blue facings, their buttonholes to be edged with narrow white tape.*[8]

But regulation uniforms were seldom in evidence. While
some States' regiments were completely uniformed, the
great majority received only sporadic issues of clothing,
and much of these were miscellaneous, nonuniform, and
of inferior quality. The average soldier wore whatever
was available.

Some of the older soldiers went to war in 1775 clothed
in the colonial regimentals they had worn during the
French wars. Some of the independent companies of the
cities, the resplendent "silk stocking companies" who
adopted the rebel cause, went to war in the uniforms
of their prewar military units. Most volunteers, however,
went out in civilian clothing and thereafter wore whatever odd items the rare issues allowed them. Only after
1780 did the Army receive any kind of regular issue of
uniform clothing, and, as deserter descriptions from
local newspapers of the time and letters and diaries confirm, even then many soldiers got no uniforms. Baron
Ludwig von Closen of the French army observed: "The
Americans suffered by comparison with our army both
in appearance and equipment, for most of these unfor-
tunates have only white cloth jackets, dirty and ragged,
and many are barefooted."[9]

In 1775, as winter approached, the Provincial Congress appealed to the citizenry for thirteen thousand
warm coats.[10] The patriotic womenfolk, sitting at their
wool-wheels and handlooms, answered the call and
supplied the order in homespun garments. In his memoirs,
the Marquis de Chastellux recalled being led into a room
"filled with the recent handiwork of Philadelphia ladies.
This work was neither embroidered waistcoats nor sets
of lace nor even gold embroidery. It was shirts for the
Pennsylvania soldiers. The ladies had provided the cloth
at their own expense and taken a real pleasure in cutting
and sewing themselves. On each shirt was marked the
name of the girl or lady who had made it, and there

128

were 2200 of them!"[11] The sight of Washington's army in their crudely made woolens elicited the sarcastic nickname "Homespuns" from the enemy English. One loyalist woman also found the wretchedly dressed rebels to present a ludicrous appearance: "I must really laugh while I recollect their figures [new recruits drilling at Wilmington, North Carolina], in their shirts and trousers, preceded by their ill-beat drum, and a fiddler who was also in his shirt with a long sword and a cue at his hair, who played with all his might. They made indeed a most unmartial appearance."[12]

Aside from the scarcity of money, the Continental troops lacked uniforms because, once they had served their term, the soldiers would take their clothing home with them. In a private dispatch to his government on 12 August 1778, the French minister Gerard stated that "the colonies are peopled with country folk in uniform, and the army is without them. It has already been provided with enough to clothe 100,000 men."[13]

Clothing scarcities, especially of shoes, plagued the Continental Army throughout the war. In an effort to alleviate the shortage, time and again numerous orders went out to the people. In 1777, for example, George Washington issued an order authorizing the impressment of all kinds of clothing, from blankets to stockings, in the areas of Bucks, Philadelphia, and Northampton.[14] In addition, advertisements such as the following were placed in the newspapers:

> *Norwich, August 7th, 1776. Wanted for the Use of the Army. A quantity of all wool, home-made cloth, suitable for soldiers coats, waistcoats, striped and plain tow cloth, linen checks, and woolen checks—also some men's shoes. All persons that have any of the said articles to spare and are willing to take a reasonable price for them, will oblige the public by bringing them to the subscriber where they may receive the cash for the same.*

Some soldiers who were lucky enough to obtain uniforms were issued captured British clothing.[15] In

Figure 4. *Men of the 2nd Virginia Regiment, 1775-1778.* The uniform shown here was modeled on the formal European-style military uniform. The small round hats cocked up on one side are fitted with military cockades of black ribbon. Their coatees, or short coats, are lapeled and cuffed in military style. They wear breeches and stockings with short leggings or spatter-dashes. The second man from the left wears soldier's "overalls"— tight, gaiter-legged trousers buttoned up halfway to the knee from the bottom.
Source: Courtesy of the Company of Military Historians, MUIA plate entitled "2nd Virginia Regiment, 1775-1778," by P. Copeland and M. Zlatich.

129

Figure 5. *Musketeer, 1776.*
White rifle frock, white overalls, and a small conical cap inscribed with "Congress," with a feather at one side. The circular device on the cap is possibly a circle of thirteen intertwined round links, each representing one of the rebellious colonies, entitled "We are one."

Source: A sketch made by a German officer, Mrs. John Nicholas Brown Collection, Providence, R.I.

other instances, their clothing was imported, most likely from France. In one case, Colonel Henry Livingston's regiment was to receive four hundred each of suits, stockings, caps, shoes, garters, and stocks. When it was discovered that Livingston had only 195 privates in his regiment at the time, only 220 hats, caps, hose, and stocks were sent. These uniforms were part of an imported lot of soldiers' clothing.[16]

As the war dragged on, the public spirit waned and volunteers no longer came forward in large numbers to enlist. Slaves were then brought in by their masters to serve in the militia. The merchants continued to demand exorbitant sums from the impoverished Congress to supply necessaries for the Army. In a letter to Washington in mid-1780, General Nathaniel Greene wrote:

> *I have made application to the merchants of this city [Philadelphia] for clothing for the Southern army; but they excused themselves, as having engaged more already than they can perform. I intend to try to put subscriptions on foot in Maryland and Virginia for the purpose of supplying clothing. Whether it will produce any good or not, time only can determine. At any rate I shall have the satisfaction of having done all in my power: and if there is not public spirit enough in the people to defend their liberties, they will deserve to be slaves.[17]*

Tragically, the clothing was sometimes available, but got lost or never reached its destination. In 1782, General Greene wrote that "not a rag of clothing has come from the northward, except a small quantity of linen for officer's shirts. A considerable quantity has been in Virginia all winter and a number of arms which we have been and still are in great want of. We have 300 men without arms, and more than a thousand men are so naked for want of clothing, that they can only be put on duty in cases of a desperate nature."[18]

The poverty-stricken conditions under which much of the Continental Army served, especially in the early

Figure 6. *Continental Marine, 1776.*
This figure is drawn from a scrimshaw carving on a powderhorn.
Source: U.S. Marine Corps Museum, Quantico, Virginia.

years of the war, are attested to in many letters and military documents that have survived. British military authorities described rebel prisoners taken in 1777 as being "almost naked, and generally without shoes—an old dirty blanket around them attached by an old leather belt around the waist."[19] George Washington reported to the President of Congress in September 1777: "At least one thousand of the men are now barefoot and have performed the late marches in that condition."[20] Albigence Waldo, a surgeon in the Continental Army, has left a picture of the American soldier that, sadly, was all too common: "There comes a soldier, his bare feet are seen through his worn-out shoes, his legs nearly naked from the tattered remains of an only pair of stockings, his breeches not sufficient to cover his nakedness, . . . he cries, . . . I am sick, my feet lame, my legs sore, my body covered with this tormenting itch."[21]

When one considers the miserable conditions under which these men had to live, the food they were given to eat—when indeed they got anything to eat at all ("perfect carrion," as one of them later described it)— it is little wonder that they deserted in the hundreds. A member of one Continental regiment remembered being issued his daily ration on Thanksgiving Day of 1777: it consisted of a half gill of rice and a tablespoon of vinegar. The soldiers were seldom paid, and when paid they received devaluated, nearly worthless Continental currency. Sickness and disease were usually rampant in the camps, and military methods of punishment were as brutal as those of the Royal Navy. And so, the Continental Army—unpaid, ill-fed, and wretchedly clothed— went on to victory and passed into history.

Figure 7. *Rifleman.*
Cloth or linen cap emblazoned with "Liberty or Death," simple civilian coat, breeches, stockings, spatterdash gaiters, and shoes—a well turned-out rebel soldier. He wears his cartridge box on his left side and has a bayonet for his musket, if not a scabbard.

　　Source: From an original print of a 1776 British caricature. Drawing by author.

Figure 8. *Soldier, 1st Independent Company, Maryland State Troops, 1776.*
Members of Maryland's seven independent companies were all dressed in similar outfits, differing primarily in color. The 1st Independent Company was issued bolts of oznabrug linen for rifle shirts and trousers. Rifles, muskets, shot pouches, cartridge boxes, powderhorns, gun flints, and bullet molds were issued, together with linen, by the Maryland Commissary of Stores in April and May 1776. Gun slings, bayonet belts, and canteens were issued the company in St. Mary's County in August 1776.

　　Source: From Manuscript Collection, Maryland Historical Society, Annapolis. Drawing by author.

Figure 9. *Soldier, Captain Samuel Evans' Company, Maryland Battalion of the Flying Camp (Middle Battalion of Militia of Cecil County), 1776.*
He is shown in typical militia man's clothing: long blue jacket, white waistcoat, and checked brown trousers. At his sides he wears a linen haversack and a tin soldier's canteen. He carries a French "Charleville" musket.
   Source: From *Pennsylvania Packet,* 12 November 1776 (deserter description). Drawing by author.

Figure 10. *Sergeant, 3rd Independent Company, Maryland State Troops, 1776.*
This rifleman is wearing a "split shirt"—a hunting shirt opening down the front and edged with fringe or ruffles. This was also known as a "Carolina shirt" and was worn by soldiers of the southern colonies. His outfit is dyed black, and he wears a straw hat. His shot bag and sergeant's sword are suspended from belts made of linen webbing instead of the scarcer leather.
   Source: From Manuscript Collection, Maryland Historical Society, Annapolis. Drawing by author.

Figure 11. *Member of a Uniformed Company of the South Carolina Militia, 1776.*
"Blue coatee with red facings, standing collar, white metal buttons, white waistcoat and breeches. Black knee bands, and gaiters (or spatterdashes), white cross belts. A beaver cap with a silver crescent in front with a black ostrich plume on the left side, and a white plume on the right, meeting at the top of the cap." Most militia companies did not have uniforms. Whether the men of this company outfitted themselves is not known.

Source: Courtesy of the Company of Military Historians Magazine, MUIA plate entitled "Soldier of the St. Helena Volunteer Company, South Carolina Militia, 1775-1776," by P. Copeland and F. McMaster.

134

Figure 12. *Soldier, 25th Continental Infantry, 1776.*
Soldiers in this company served aboard Arnold's fleet at Lake
Champlain in 1776. Here we see seaman's dress, jacket, vest,
and trousers, an uncocked round hat and Indian moccasins.
He carries a short rampart gun, used aboard armed boats of
the time.
  Source: From the Smithsonian Institution, Museum of
History and Technology, Washington, D.C. Drawing by author.

Figure 13. *Soldier, 10th Continental Regiment, Connecticut, 1776.*
Light brown coat with red lining and facings, light brown waist-
coat, and buckskin leather breeches. His coat buttons are of
pewter, marked with the regimental number "10."
  Source: From the Smithsonian Institution, Museum of
History and Technology, Washington, D.C. Drawing by author.

Figure 14. *Private, 1st Regiment Continental Line, 1776.*
This soldier wears the hunting shirt and overalls that Washington prescribed in 1775 as the uniform of the Army. His round hat is of castor felt, and at his waist he wears a long sheath knife. He carries a hatchet or camp axe in lieu of a bayonet. His overalls are gartered at the knee.
Source: From the Smithsonian Institution, Museum of History and Technology, Washington, D.C. Drawing by author.

Figure 15. *Continental Marine, 1776.*
A description of this marine is from a newspaper of the time: "Deserted from Captain William Shippin's Company of Marines belonging to the Brig Hancock, Joseph Bamford, . . 30 years of age, 5 feet 7 or 8 inches high . . . Had on an old blue coatee, old leather breeches, a check shirt, and an old felt hat."
Source: From *Pennsylvania Evening Post,* 1 June 1776. Drawing by author.

Figure 16. *Rifleman, 4th Pennsylvania Battalion, 1776.*
Instead of rifle dress, this soldier wears patched and worn out
remnants of the regimental uniform issued him in early 1776.
His cocked hat has been cut down to become a small round
hat; his coat, dark blue with white facings, has had the skirts
cut off and has become a coatee. His shoes and stockings have
worn out, and he is barefoot, a not uncommon condition of
the Continental Army.
    Source: Courtesy of the Company of Military Historians
Magazine, MUIA plate entitled "Soldier of the Rifle Company,
4th Pennsylvania Battalion, 1776," by P. Copeland.

Figure 17. *Soldier, 5th Worcester County Regiment,
Massachusetts, 1776.*
This rural militia man is well-clothed and -equipped com-
pared to many soldiers of the Continental regiments. He wears
a neat suit of homespun cloth, made up and dyed by the women
of his family; a round felt hat decorated by a cockade and
sprig of fir; and an old-style British leather accoutrement
belt from which hangs a camp axe, or tomahawk, in lieu of a
bayonet.
    Source: Copeland, *Everyday Dress of the American
Revolution.*

137

Figure 18. *Member of the 5th Pennsylvania Battalion, 1776.* Brown coat with red facings and white lining, white waistcoat, leather breeches, and rattlesnake skin hat band in an uncocked, round hat.

Source: "Brother Jonathan, Soldier of the American Revolution," print series, by Peter Copeland and Donald W. Holst.

138

Figure 19. *Member of the 1st Company of Maryland Mattrosses, 1776.*
This artillery company ("mattross" is the ancient name for gunner or artilleryman) guarded the approaches to Baltimore. The uniform of the 1st Company consisted of blue coats faced and lined in white, grey waistcoats and leather breeches, and white metal buttons.
   Source: "Brother Jonathan."

139

Figure 20. *Member of the Boys' Company, 1775.*
Hunting shirts emblazoned with the popular patriotic motto "Liberty or Death" across the front, trousers, and small round hats caught up on one side with cockade and buck's tail. The Boys' Company was armed with Indian trade muskets, the stocks of which were painted blue. These guns were plundered from the magazine at Williamsburg, seen in the background here.
    Source: "Brother Jonathan."

Figure 21. *Member of the Delaware Battalion of the Flying Camp, 1776.*

The only attempt at uniform dress adopted was a light blue cockade of ribbon worn in each man's hat, presumably to distinguish the Battalion of the Flying Camp from other Delaware units. The Delaware militia man wears over his single-breasted civilian coat a blanket roll (in lieu of a knapsack) and a linen haversack. He has an old-style military tin canteen and a powderhorn.

Source: "Brother Jonathan."

141

Figure 22. *Soldier, 1777.*
This drawing is based on an illustration on an old piece of war-time paper currency issued by the State of Delaware in 1777. He wears a round-bottomed, belted waistcoat without skirts, a round hat decorated by a buck's tail, and a proper regimental coat.
   Source: Drawing by author.

Figure 23. *Two Artificers, Continental Army, 1778-1779.*
The Artificer on the left wears the winter issue; the man on the right wears the linen frock and overalls of the 1779 issue.
   Source: From *Jacob Weiss Letter Book*, Library of Congress, Washington, D.C. Drawing by author.

Figure 24. *Soldier, 7th Virginia Regiment, 1777.*
The first issue of clothing to the 7th Virginia Regiment consisted of black-fringed rifle shirts and brown linen leggings. Most of the regiment wore large, round, coarse felt hats, uncocked. This soldier carries a cartridge box on a white duck belt, a keg-type wooden canteen, and a coarse linen haversack.
    Source: "Brother Jonathan."

Figure 25. *Soldier, 1st Connecticut Regiment, 1778.*
The coat shown here (red in color) was popular among Connecticut soldiers, despite apparent confusion with the British uniforms. Several Connecticut regiments wore red coats until late in the war. The men of the 1st Connecticut wore small round hats rather than the conventional cocked hat of the European foot soldier.
    Source: "Brother Jonathan."

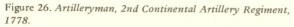

Figure 26. *Artilleryman, 2nd Continental Artillery Regiment, 1778.*

The *New York Journal* described this man as having run away from his regiment wearing "a brown coat with red facings, a red and white striped waistcoat, blue and white striped trousers, and a felt hat."

Source: From *New York Journal*, 25 May 1778. Drawing by author.

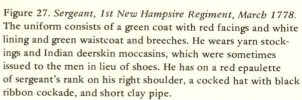

Figure 27. *Sergeant, 1st New Hampsire Regiment, March 1778.*
The uniform consists of a green coat with red facings and white lining and green waistcoat and breeches. He wears yarn stockings and Indian deerskin moccasins, which were sometimes issued to the men in lieu of shoes. He has on a red epaulette of sergeant's rank on his right shoulder, a cocked hat with black ribbon cockade, and short clay pipe.
Source: "Brother Jonathan."

Figure 28. *Illinois Regiment, Virginia State Forces, 1778-1781.*
The soldier in the left foreground wears the rifle dress common
to the American frontier and worn by the regiment prior to
the adoption of a more formal uniform in 1780. The soldier
on the far right is dressed in a dark blue coatee with white
facings, dark blue vest, and overalls. The officer has a formal
brown coat with red facings, grey vest, and breeches. The inter-
preter wears an Indian coat over his uniform.

Source: Courtesy of the Company of Military Historians,
MUIA plate entitled "The Illinois Regiment, 1778-1781," by
Peter Copeland and Marko Zlatich.

Figure 29. *Fifer, 2nd Continental Artillery Regiment, 1779.*
The fifer is attired in the prescribed uniform for fifes and drums (reversed colors): red coat faced with black and white lining, yellow buttons and lace, white waistcoat and breeches, white stockings, and black spatterdashes. The drums and fifes wore small round hats with silver cord, edged with yellow lace, with a tuft of bearskin above the cockade.
   Source: "Brother Jonathan."

Figure 30. *American Soldier in Rifle Dress, 1780.*
These contemporary German drawings show a leather cap emblazoned with the word "Congress" and with a plume or feather at the side. The soldier's coarse cotton rifle frock and trousers are dark blue-grey with white decorative fringes. His long hair is clubbed behind. His belts are of brown leather, and his cartridge box is of black leather.
   Source: American Heritage Book of the Revolution (New York, 1958), p. 165.

146

Figure 31. *Massachusetts Soldier, 1781.*
The soldier's uniform is that adopted for the Massachusetts line by the committee of officers of the Review Board of Massachusetts. It conforms to the Board of War's regulations regarding the color to be worn for Massachusetts troops: blue faced with white. A detailed description of this uniform, specifying number and size of buttons on lapel and cuff, width of lapel, length of skirt, and the like, may be found in Elizabeth McClellan's *History of American Costume* (Philadelphia, 1904), p. 365.

Figure 32. *Officer, 3rd Regiment of Continental Light Dragoons, 1781.*
The 3rd Regiment's prescribed uniform consisted of white coats faced and lined in blue, white waistcoats, and leather breeches. The turban bound about the helmet was also blue, and the crest of the helmet brass, with white horsehair decoration; a black ostrich plume surmounted the crest.
    Source: "Brother Jonathan."

Figure 33. *British Sentry in Canadian Winter Clothing, 1777.*
He wears a red cap with brown fur turban and tail; white capote
(or blanket coat) with hood; and light blue trim on cuffs and
hem. A light blue rosette is on the hip and light blue string or
tape is visible on the breast. His blue leggings (or trousers) have
at least seven buttons down the side. He has a black bayonet
scabbard on his white waist belt, black cartridge box, and
white shoulder belt.

    Source: From Albert W. Haarman and Donald W. Holst,
"The Friedrich von Germann Drawings of Troops in the American Revolution," *Military Collector and Historian* (Spring
1964). Drawing by author.

Figure 34. *Corporal, Rhode Island Regiment, 1781.*
The corporal has on a short white jacket with red cuffs, white
waistcoat, and overalls of unbleached linen. His cap is probably
made of black leather with a white binding on the front flap.
The device of Rhode Island—an anchor in white—is on the
front. His buttons are of lead or pewter, and his corporal's
epaulette is green worsted.
    Source: Copeland, *Uniforms of the American Revolution,*
drawing by Baron Ludwig von Closen, von Closen Papers,
Manuscript Division, Library of Congress, Washington, D.C.

NOTES

1. John Fitzpatrick, ed., *The Writings of George Washington*
   (Washington, D.C., 1931), Vol. 1, p. 176.
2. Earle, *Two Centuries of Costume in America,* p. 695.
3. Fitzpatrick, op. cit., Vol. 3.
4. *Public Advertiser* (London, 13 March 1776).
5. Earle, op. cit., p. 698.
6. *Newport Mercury Extraordinary* (11 July 1776); *Providence
   Gazette* (29 July 1776).
7. *Purdie's Virginia Gazette* (10 May 1776).
8. Board of War Regulations, 1779.
9. *The Unpublished Journal of Baron von Closen* (Washington,
   D.C., n.d.).
10. Earle, op. cit., p. 694.
11. *Voyages de M. le Marquis de Chastellux dans l'Amerique
    Septentrionale* (Paris, 1788).
12. Janet Shaw, ed., *Journal of a Lady of Quality, Being a
    Narrative of a Journey from Scotland to the West Indies,
    North Carolina, and Portugal in the Years 1774-1776*
    (New Haven, 1927), p. 281.
13. Sherrill, *French Memories of 18th Century America.*
14. Fitzpatrick, op. cit., Vol. 9.
15. *The Papers of George Washington* (Washington, D.C.),
    Vol. 188.
16. *Minutes, Charles Thomson, Secretary, Pennsylvania Archives,*
    1st Series, Vol. VII (Philadelphia, 1853), p. 221-223.
17. Jared Sparks, *Correspondence of the American Revolution*
    (Boston, 1853), Vol. 3, pp. 137-139.
18. *Papers of the Continental Congress* (National Archives),
    Vol. 2, folios 433-439, item 155.
19. A report from British headquarters to London, 1777.
20. Fitzpatrick, op. cit., Vol. 3.
21. Charles K. Bolton, *The Private Soldier Under Washington*
    (New York, 1902).

(9)
Professionals

As in England, the sons in the middle and upper classes of colonial America had a choice of the legal or medical professions and the ministry. Beginning in the eighteenth century, America began to build an independent reputation in these professions. The century witnessed the establishment of several native law and medical schools and a revival of religious interest, and, as in business and agriculture, the colonists were becoming less and less dependent on the mother country in the areas of the law, medicine, and religion.

At the start of the century, medical knowledge in the colonies was on a par with that in Western Europe, primarily because most of America's physicians were trained in foreign medical schools such as the Universities of Edinburgh, Leyden, and Paris and at London lectures. It was not until after the middle of the century that medical schools were established in the colonies. Among the first colleges were the Medical Faculty of the College of Philadelphia (1765) and King's College (1767).

One of the main differences between the colonial and English doctors was that the colonists practiced more generalized medicine. That is, whereas in England the physician, surgeon, and apothecary formed roughly separate branches of medicine, in America the physician performed all three functions.[1]

As was the case with medicine, there were few native law schools until after 1750. The first law lectures were not instituted until 1779—at William and Mary. In the 1780s and 1790s, law schools were established at Litchfield, Connecticut, Kinderbrook, New York, Pennsylvania, and Columbia.

As regards religion, during the eighteenth century many additional sects came to the colonies, including the Presbyterians, Dunkards, Moravians, Methodists, Shakers, Universalists, and the German Reformed. Already firmly based from the 1600s were the Anglicans, Lutherans, Baptists, Quakers, Congregationalists, Mennonites, and the Dutch Reformed. As was true of law and medicine, several theological colleges were established and began to flourish toward the last quarter

Figure 1. *American Surgeon, 1770s.*
Cocked hat bound in black ferret, ruffled shirt of white linen,
close-bodied, single-breasted black coat with silver buttons,
black breeches, white silk stockings, silver buckles, silver-headed
cane, and white, full-bottomed "physical wig."

Source: Copeland, *Everyday Dress of the American
Revolution.*

of the century. The first among them was at New
Brunswick, New Jersey.

DRESS

In most cases, the occupations represented in this
chapter dressed in the style of the period, much as did
all other middle-class people.

Physicians

Physicians favored plain suits made up in a dark
color, most often black. In common with members of
other "learned professions," doctors usually wore
"physical wigs" (physician's wigs), which were white
and bushy and sometimes worn with a short queue.[2]
The typical physician of the second half of the century
wore a suit of black velvet, a ruffled white linen shirt,
a full-bottomed wig, and a cocked hat. As did any
middle-class gentleman until the latter years of the
century, he carried a sword and favored a gold- or
silver-headed cane. He had a muff when abroad (another
middle-class affectation of the mid-century) and wore
shoes with silver buckles. Doctors in rural areas were
not able to match this sartorial elegance; their dress
was closer to that of well-to-do farmers.

Dr. Alexander Hamilton has left us a rather amusing
picture of an American doctor in 1744: "There was
among the rest, a doctor, a tall, thin man about whom
nothing appeared remarkable but his dress. He had a
weather beaten black wig, and an old striped collimancoe
banyan, and an antique brass spur on his right ankle,
and a pair of thick soald shoes tied with points."[3]
Many physicians continued to wear wigs until well
into the nineteenth century, long after they had gone
out of fashion.

English apothecaries were clothed in the middle-class
fashion of the time. Occasionally, their working dress
was augmented by a blue apron and protective sleeves
like those worn by butchers.

Lawyers

Members of the legal profession in England wore a

152

distinctive costume in the court room, a custom that was carried to America. In both countries, the judge wore a scarlet gown (originally to denote a Crown official), and lawyers wore black robes. A visitor to the Supreme Court at the State House in Philadelphia in 1787 described the judges as being dressed in wigs and scarlet robes; he noted with surprise that the Chief Judge sat on a bench with his hat on. Apparently, use of a hat while in session was not all that uncommon: it is recorded that when the court held sessions at Harrisburg, Pennsylvania, in 1777-1778 the Chief Judge also wore his hat.[4]

The proper appearance of magistrates in their ceremonial robes was of no little interest to the people. Witness the contempt of this writer in 1747 who was appalled by the slovenly habits of one New York City magistrate:

> *To see an alderman sit or stand in the seat of justice and award payment of 5 shillings six-pence to a person of his ward that comes to him for relief, in the pompous robe of a greasy woolen cap and a tattered Banjann [Banyan] jacket, must certainly commend the greatest respect, both to their knowledge and good manners. Yet I have seen one of these robed magistrates vouchsafe to powder his wig and put it on, without quitting his Banjann, to sup with one of the Ward upon the profits of his daily labour, provided the feast was graced with some good oysters, a pipe of tobbacco and a mug of strong beer. I am not for becoming a slave to the fashion, or making dress the whole business of my life; though at the same time, I think that every person that appears in public, clothed in authority, should be decent and clean . . . I will venture to affirm no magistrate ever lost a vote by putting on a clean shirt when he was dirty, or clothing the seat of his brain with a powdered wig instead of a dirty cap.*[5]

Figure 2. *American Doctor of Civil Law, 1790s.*
The color of his robes presumably is black. This formal academic gown, worn with bands, is not very different from that of an Anglican cleric of the time. A portrait of John Jay, first Chief Justice of the United States Supreme Court, shows him clad in similar robes, which are described as being of black silk faced with red satin and edged in white.
Source: From McClellan, *Historic Dress in America.* Drawing by author.

153

Figure 3. *Lord Mayor of London and Alderman, 1750s.*
The Lord Mayor wears a wig; the alderman wears his own hair,
unpowdered, curled at the side, and tied behind in a queue.
The mayor's coat and waistcoat are embroidered at the edges.
Source: Anonymous print in the author's collection.

*The Right Honble Brass Crosby Esqr Lord Mayor,
and Richd Oliver Esqr Alderman of London*

Clergymen

Ministers of the various religions in colonial America usually wore plain black suits with a clergyman's band at the throat, both on weekdays and on the Sabbath. They eschewed the use of gowns, cassocks, or surplices, either in the pulpit or on the street. In the main, the objection to religious gowns was that they smacked too much of the hated Papists and Episcopalians.[6] The theme of many a sermon in the colonial period centered on the deplorable use of clerical gowns in the pulpit. (For several portraits of religious gowns as worn by the Anglican Divines and Catholic priests, see Elizabeth McClellan, *Historic Dress in America,* pp. 308-310.)

The parish beadle, whose duties it was to preserve order during services and to act as church usher, wore the conventional middle-class fashions: cocked hat, single-breasted coat, waistcoat, and breeches.

154

Figure 4. *Two English Judges, 1758.*
Both wear long, full wigs, scarlet robes edged with gold, and full white sleeves. Their robes are fastened at the waist with knotted ribbons. At their throats are bands like those of clerics.
Source: William Hogarth, "The Bench," 1758.

Figure 5. *Anglican Clergyman, 1785.*
This black wide-sleeved academic-type gown was usually worn over a plain black suit. The black round hat was bound with black ribbon, which was knotted at the side. The clerical bands worn at the throat were white.
Source: Two prints in the author's collection, by John Kay, 1785 and 1798. Drawing by author.

155

Drawn & Engraved by Abner Reed, 1808 — from an Original Portrait by Mr. King.

Rev. GARDNER THURSTON.

Died Aug. 23, 1802 — — — — Aged 81 Yrs.

Figure 6. *English Clergyman, Circa 1800.*
He wears no clerical bands. He has on a simple black suit and
a full-bodied "physical wig."
   Source: A print in the author's collection, engraved by
Abner Reed, dated 1808.

156

Figure 7. *Beadle of Saffron Hill, Hatton Gardens, and Ely Rents, London, Circa 1750.*
Tinsel-edged cocked hat, close-bodied, single-breasted coat with edged pockets, waistcoat, and breeches with ties at the knee. His coat has slashed sleeves rather than cuffs. He wears the type of neck cloth or cravat commonly worn in the first half of the eighteenth century.

Source: A print in the author's collection, engraved by R. Grave, undated.

NOTES

1. Ver Steeg, *The Formative Years,* p. 241.
2. Cunnington, Lucas, and Mansfield, *Occupational Costume in England,* p. 305.
3. *A Gentleman's Progress: The Itinerarium of Dr. Alexander Hamilton, 1744* (Chapel Hill, N.C., 1948).
4. Elizabeth McClellan, *Historic Dress in America* (Philadelphia, 1904), pp. 335-339.
5. Singleton, *Social New York Under the Georges.*
6. Earle, *Two Centuries of Costume in America,* p. 415.

(10)
House Servants

In the eighteenth century, domestic servants were not exclusively had by the wealthy. A farmer living on his own land, or even a small tradesman or shopkeeper, kept at least one domestic servant in his household. There were numerous sources for this labor. Large farmers and merchants often purchased the labor of servants and recent immigrants indentured from England for a set period of years. People from the lower classes hired themselves out to domestic service. Also, many planters and farmers used their most clever Negro slaves as house servants.

DRESS

In small households, servants dressed in ordinary working class clothing, supplied by the master of the house. In larger and grander households, servants dressed in livery, a custom dating back to the Middle Ages. Livery, a uniform dress given servants, was sometimes functional (as for kitchen workers) and sometimes ornamental (as for footmen or coachmen). Some servants of wealthy houses, especially young page boys, were clothed in gaudy and fantastical dress. Livery clothing would usually be made up in the colors of the master's armorial bearings. Thus it was that George Washington dressed his house servants in scarlet and white, the colors found in his family's coat of arms.

A suit of livery in a wealthy family would consist of a coat, waistcoat, and breeches, all done in the fashion of the day. They would often be embellished with lace or binding of a distinctive pattern or color, in much the same style as the clothing issued to soldiers. Cocked hats and, in climates where necessary, overcoats completed the servant's livery. These garments were sometimes so elegant as to cause confusion in the eyes of strangers as to the station of the servants. As one of the dramas of the century so aptly put it: "Livery? Lord, Madam, I took him for a Captain, he's so bedizned with lace! And then he has tops on his shoes up to his mid leg. . . and has a fine long periwig tied up in a bag."[1]

A London newspaper of 1777 described the footmen

Figure 1. *Colonial Servant Girl, 1775.*
She wears a kerchief knotted about her head, decorated with
a flower, plaid shawl over her shoulders and covering her bodice,
and patched white linen or cotton apron tied about her waist.
Like most working women, her dress is worn without hoops.

 Source: Copeland, *Everyday Dress of the American
Revolution.*

of Lord Derby with their "red feathers, and flame colored
stockings" as looking like creatures out of an opera.
An American observer described the livery dress he saw
in England at the end of the century: "They wore lace
[braid] not only on the borders but on all the seams
of their garments, and their large cocked hats were
surrounded by broad fringes of silver and gold."[2] This
dress was much like that of the fifers, drummers, and
bandsmen in some of the more ornate regiments of
Great Britain and other European countries throughout
the century. Another point of similarity between livery
dress and the military uniform was the shoulder knot,
which was worn by some servants in livery. For most
of the eighteenth century, the shoulder knot was also
the insignia of an officer and was part of his uniform
dress. For both the servant and the soldier it derived
from a common source—service to the nobility.

 In some houses in America, the Negro slaves were
also dressed in livery. In a letter to Charles Laurence,
written in 1764, George Washington described the livery
dress of his servants:

> *A livery suit to be made of worsted shagg
> of the inclosed colour and fineness lined with
> red shalloon; and made as follows; The coat and
> breeches alike with a plain white washed button;
> the button holes worked with mohair of the
> same colour. A collar of red shagg to the coat
> with a narrow lace like the inclosed round it.
> A narrow cuff of the same colour of the coat
> turned up to the bend of the arm and laced
> round that part; the waistcoat made of red
> shagg (worsted shagg also) and laced with the
> same lace as that upon the collar and sleeves.
> This suit to be made by the largest measure
> sent and charged to George Washington.
> Also one other livery suit made exactly as
> the above and of the same colour shaggs and
> lace by the other measure but charged to
> Master Custis.*[3]

160

The colonial aristocrats ordered almost all the manufactured goods required for clothing their families and servants from Great Britain. In a letter to Mary Washington, dated 1757, Washington stated:

> *I have waited till now, expecting the arrival*
> *of my negros cloaths from Great Britain; but*
> *as the season is advancing and risks attending*
> *them I can no longer depend, and therefor*
> *beg the favor of you to choose me about 250*
> *yds. of Oznebergs 200 yds. of cotton 35 pr*
> *Plad Hoes [plaid hose] and as much thread*
> *as is necessary in Lewis' store if he has them*
> *if not in Mr. Jackson's and send them up by*
> *Jno who comes down with a Tumbler for that*
> *purpose.*[4]

Even during the lean war years, when supplies of cloth of any kind were exceedingly scarce, Washington, as commander of the Continental Army, tried to clothe his servants in something approaching livery dress. In a letter from Morristown, New Jersey, to Caleb Gibbs in May 1777, he requested cloth and trimmings for suits of clothing for his servant, Will, and for his hostler: "Get Russia drill enough to make each two waistcoats and two pairs of breeches. The coats may be made of a light coloured cloth of any kind, lined with red shalloon. A bit of red cloth for capes or collars to them."[5]

Servants in the wealthy colonial houses were probably in livery and cocked hats if the family was wealthy listing the household effects offered for sale upon the death of Governor Montgomerie of New York in 1731. Among the goods sold were "some blew cloth lately come from London for Liveries; some white drap cloth with proper trimming. Some broad gold lace."[6]

A prosperous household in both England and America kept at least a couple of footmen, a coachman, and a postillion, in addition to butlers, valets, and maids. The footmen, coachman, and postillion would also be dressed in livery and cocked hats if the family was wealthy enough. The Duke of Bedford paid almost five pounds

Figure 2. *English Lady's Maid, Circa 1760.*
Linen cap, a gown open in front with criss-cross lacing over the corset front, and winged cuffs.
    Source: From "Pride," by James McArdell, after C. A. Coypel, London, circa 1760; M. C. Salaman, *Old English Mezzotints* (London, 1910). Drawing by author.

161

Trinkt nun ihr die Milch, Gott hat sie euch beschneden
Torstendalds Geschichte von Kayser

Figure 3. *German Serving Woman, 1790s.*
Linen cap, short gown, kerchief about her neck, and apron.
   Source: A print in the author's collection, by I. F. de Goetz, 1797.

apiece (almost two months' pay for a skilled working man of the time) for the livery dress of his postillions. They were in orange uniform, richly laced with gold and velvet and bespangled with gilt buttons. Late in the century, as part of their livery, coachmen wore surtout coats called "wrap rascals" which had many overlapping capes to keep out the rain. The coachmen, stable boys, undergrooms, postillions, and hostlers received linen frocks for wear in the stables, while working on the horses—as indeed would all servants for rough and dirty work.[7] Unlike the coachmen and postillions, however, stable boys, undergrooms, and hostlers were never issued livery. For ordinary wear they dressed simply in loose brown jackets or short coatees, breeches, gaiters, waistcoats, and round hats or caps.[8]

One of the most elaborately dressed servants was the running footman, whose duty it was to run before his master's coach. A running footman of Ireland in the 1760s was described as wearing a white jacket with a sash of blue silk, a velvet cap, and long staff. An English footman of 1730 wore "fine Holland drawers and waistcoat, a blue sash, fringed with silver, a velvet cap with a great tassel, and a porter's staff with a large silver handle."[9] The "fine Holland drawers" were linen petticoat trousers, like those worn by seamen. They were part of the running footman's uniform throughout the century.

The "upper class" of house servants— butlers and valets—was dressed, not in livery, but in gentleman's dress, much like that of their masters. A visitor to the Duke of Newcastle in 1780 observed: "Ten or twelve servants out of livery attended on us, which would naturally make it difficult for a stranger to distinguish between the guests and the servants."[10] Such dress was usually conservative and not in the very latest fashion, however. For example, upper class servants wore wigs long after they were fashionable.

Women servants were clothed according to their rank in the household rather than in livery. This custom also caused confusion. In 1725, Daniel Defoe explained how he was "once put very much to blush, being at a

162

friend's house and required of him to salute the ladies, I kissed the Chamber-Made into the bargain, for she was as well dressed as the best. Things of this kind would be avoided if our servant maids were to wear livery as our footmen do, or if they were obliged to go in a dress suitable to their station."[11] In many great houses chamber maids and waiting women sometimes dressed quite as well as their mistresses: they too wore silk petticoats, cambric head cloths, fine Holland linen, and silk or cotton stockings. One housekeeper was described in 1745 as wearing a tied-up mob cap and a decorative apron—just what an upper class lady would wear when at home.

For a description of how a rural maiden was transformed upon entering service in a wealthy household we are again indebted to Defoe:

> Her neats leather shoes are now transformed into laced shoes with high heels; her yarn stockings are turned into fine worsted ones with silk clocks; her wooden pattens are kicked away for leathern clogs; she must have a hoop too . . . and her poor scanty linsey woolsey petticoat is changed into a good silk one four or five yards wide.

The typical dress of the English maid was slightly less elaborate: calico or linen frock with worsted petticoat; long white apron; kerchief of muslin; mob cap trimmed with ribbon; and Spanish leather shoes. The skirt of her frock ended just above her ankles.[12]

In the smaller households of colonial America, servants were clothed much more modestly. Typically, their dress consisted of buckskin breeches, flannel shirt, jacket, hat or cap, waistcoat, shoes, stockings, and perhaps a kerchief. This was, of course, also the typical working class dress of the time; thus, such servants were indistinguishable from street laborers. The colonial servant girl's dress is described in an ad from the *Pennsylvania Gazette* (1773):

Figure 4. *French Housemaid, Circa 1740.*
White linen cap, white blouse, light brown skirt, and green apron. Her shoes are old fashioned in cut, in the style of the beginning of the century.
    Source: From "La Pourvoyeuse," oil on canvas, by Chardin, 1740, The Louvre. Drawing by author.

163

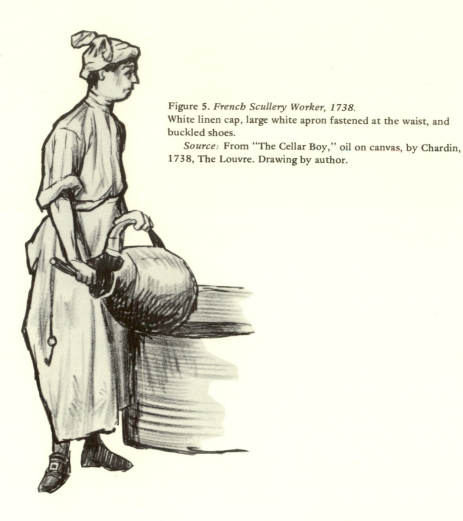

Figure 5. *French Scullery Worker, 1738.*
White linen cap, large white apron fastened at the waist, and buckled shoes.
   Source: From "The Cellar Boy," oil on canvas, by Chardin, 1738, The Louvre. Drawing by author.

Ran away from the subscriber, an English servant girl named Christiana Ball, but calls herself Caty for shortness, about twenty years of age, brown skinned, black eyes, and hair lately cut short, a little stoop shouldered. Her cloaths are very ordinary, a brown cloth petticoat, other coarse shifts and a striped calico short gown.

In general, English servants were considered to be inferior to those brought over from the Continent. The primary reason was that the English were too independent to adapt easily to service. This spirit of independence harked back to their experiences in England. It has been noted that if a master struck his servant in England, the servant just might be liable to knock him down. As for English maidservants, they wished to dress in the same mode as their mistresses and to amuse themselves in the same manner. Judging from the large number of English, Scots, and Irish named in colonial newspapers throughout the century, the Britons who came to the colonies as indentured servants were as ill fitted for the tasks of service in the New World as they had been in the Old.

Figure 6. *Young Black Slave Page, England, 1740s.*
He is attired in a turban decorated with feather and beads and an engraved silver collar about his neck—a decorative badge of slavery. His dress is servant's livery, in the colors of the family he serves. The buttonholes of his coat are embroidered with metallic lace. He wears a knot of ribbons at the rear of his shoulder. His shirt is of fine Holland linen, ruffled at the throat.
   Source: Copeland, op. cit.

Figure 7. *Slave Footman of Mount Vernon, 1765.*
His coat is off-white with red cuffs and collar, his breeches are white, and his waistcoat is red; the coat has a red lining. The waistcoat, cuffs, and collar are edged with red and white banding. His stockings are plaid, and his shoes have coarse metal buckles, as do the knees of his breeches. His round hat is cocked up and edged with white tape. His coat is without outside pockets, though there may have been inner pockets.
   Source: Copeland, op. cit.

Figure 8. *Black Servant of Mount Vernon, Mid-1790s.*
This servant, shown in the livery dress of the Washington family, wears the double-breasted straight-bottomed waistcoat of the period. The cape of his coat is large, and the coat sleeve ends in a small tight cuff. His coat and waistcoat are light colored. The lining of his waistcoat and the cape and cuff of his coat are red.

Source: From "The Washington Family," oil on canvas, by Edward Savage, 1796, National Gallery of Art, Washington, D.C., courtesy of Albert Haarman. Drawing by author.

Figure 9. *Black Servant of the Duke of Cumberland, Circa 1760.*
White turban embroidered with gold stripes, crimson coat with
green cuffs and lining, green waistcoat and breeches.

 Source: From a watercolor drawing by Paul Sandby, in
A. P. Oppé, *The Drawings of Paul and Thomas Sandby in the
Collection of His Majesty the King at Windsor Castle.* Drawing
by author.

Figure 10. *English Footman, 1792.*
He wears a light-colored coat with dark cuffs, ornately laced
coat, ruffled shirt of fine linen, and neck cloth at his throat.
His waistcoat and breeches are of a dark color, probably the
same color as the cuffs of his coat. His stockings are white, and
his shoes are buckled. His hair is curled and powdered.

 Source: A print in the author's collection, entitled "Dumps
the Footman," by de Wilde, London, 1792.

Figure 11. *Slave Manservant of the Calvert Family of Maryland, 1761.*

He is in the livery of the Calverts and wears a coat, vest, and breeches of yellow cloth. The cape and cuffs of his coat are black, and the edges of his coat and vest are laced in yellow and black.

Source: From "Charles Calvert and Negro Servant," by John Hessallius, oil on canvas, 1761, courtesy of Mrs. C. C. DeCato, Baltimore Museum of Art. Drawing by author.

Figure 12. *Manservant to the Marquis de Lafayette, 1781.*
The dress of this servant is a variation of the military uniform of the time: round hat decorated with black and white ostrich feathers; single-breasted jacket edged with metallic lace; white linen cravat; striped sash; gaiter-legged trousers, fitting closely to the leg like a common soldier's overalls; and short, laced up boots, similar to those worn by some German and Austrian military units of the time.

Source: From a print entitled "Conclusion de la Campagne de 1781 en Virginie," appearing in *Les Combattants Français de la Guerre Americaine, 1778-1783,* published by Ministere des Affaires Etrangeres (Paris, 1903); the painting "Marquis de Lafayette at Yorktown," by Jean-Baptiste le Paon, 1783. Drawing by author.

168

Figure 13. *English Horse Groom in Livery, Circa 1798.*
Long single-breasted coat, the collar and cuffs of which are
edged with lace; black hat with white band and black cockade;
leather belt about his waist; and hunting horn on a strap over
his shoulder. He is booted and spurred and carries a crop.
  Source: From "Charger with a Groom," by George Stubbs,
1798, oil on canvas, Mellon Collection, Washington, D.C.
Drawing by author.

Figure 14. *French Chef to the Duke of Newcastle, England,
Circa 1750-1755.*
Kerchief knotted about his head, black neck cloth, white
jacket and apron, breeches and stockings.
  Source: From a print entitled "Cloue, Chef to the Duke
of Newcastle," *Horizon* (November 1958): 57. Drawing by
author.

Figure 15. *English Stable Boy, 1760s.*
White linen shirt, checked waistcoat, leather breeches, and black stockings.

    Source: From "Gimcrack," by George Stubbs, 1764, oil on canvas. Drawing by author.

Figure 16. *Two French Gardeners, 1794.*
The man with the rake wears a white linen cap, shirt, and an under waistcoat of white cut straight across the bottom without skirts. His light brown outer waistcoat is sleeveless with short skirts. His trousers are pale blue-grey. The other gardener wears a round white hat, white linen shirt, pale brown waistcoat with short skirts, and pale blue-grey trousers.

    Source: From "Le Jardin des Plantes," by Jean Baptiste Hilair, 1794, a watercolor, Bibliotheque Nationale, Paris. Drawing by author.

NOTES

1. George Farquhar, *The Beaux Stratagem* (1707).
2. Cunnington, Lucas, and Mansfield, *Occupational Costume in England.*
3. Fitzpatrick, *The Writings of George Washington,* Vol. 2.
4. Ibid., Vol. 2.
5. Ibid., Vol. 3.
6. Earle, *Two Centuries of Costume in America.*
7. Cunnington, Lucas, and Mansfield, op. cit.
8. Ibid.
9. *Weekly Journal* (London, 1730).
10. Cunnington, Lucas, and Mansfield, op. cit.
11. Ibid.
12. Ibid.

(11)
Indentured Servants and Slaves

The growth of the economy in the seventeenth century created a demand for cheap labor. This demand was filled by various forms of voluntary and involuntary bondage, namely, white indentured service and black slavery. In the early years, most of the indentured servants came to the southern colonies. Between 1664 and 1671, it has been estimated that a total of 10,500 such servants migrated to Virginia alone, and by 1700 Maryland had an equal number of indentured servants and slaves. As many as half of all white migrants to the New World may have come under bondage.[1] It was only in the eighteenth century that slavery replaced indentured service as the primary source of labor in the southern colonies. At this time, indentured servants began to populate the middle colonies where, upon fulfillment of their labor agreements, they found cheaper land opportunities.

There were a number of sources for the indentured labor force. One source was the poor (often Germans) who traveled to the American colonies without a labor contract and spent a number of years in servitude in return for their passage to the New World. In some cases, relatives or friends came forth with the required cost of their passage, and bailed some redemptioners out, but the vast majority had to sell themselves into a term of bondage in payment for their voyage. Another source was comprised of those (usually the Scotch-Irish) who, unable to pay their passage to America, signed a contract of indenture before leaving England. Once the redemptioner entered indenture upon the deck of a ship in an American port, he became an indentured bondsman and, like the black slave, became the property of his owner.

The usual cost of transporting a redemptioner to the New World was about ten pounds, and he fetched from fifteen to as much as forty or fifty pounds from a prospective master, the amount depending on his or her skills. The ship's captain thus pocketed a tidy profit, while the new master recieved at least four years of labor at no cost except that of housing, clothing, and feeding his bondsman.[2]

Convicts supplied another portion of the indentured

Figure 1. *Pennsylvania Slave, 1730.*
This runaway was described to be wearing "a new oznabrug shirt and a pair of striped homespun breeches, a striped ticking waistcoat, and old dimity coat of his masters with buttons or horse teeth set in brass and cloth sleeves and a felt hat almost new."

Source: From *Pennsylvania Gazette,* No. 91, August 1730. Drawing by author.

labor force. Most of these were English criminals who were given the choice of bondage in the colonies or harsh prison sentences (often the gallows) in their native country. Some of these convicts were serious offenders; others were political prisoners, such as the Highland Scots families who were transported for participating in the Jacobite rebellion of 1745. During the eighteenth century, forty to sixty thousand felons migrated to America, principally to Maryland, Virginia, and Georgia. These convicts were sold into colonial servitude for a minimum of seven years and a maximum of fourteen.

Finally, labor for the American colonies was obtained through kidnapping. A favorite method of kidnapping was similar to that used by waterfront "crimps" operating out of seamen's boarding houses. The victims were plied with liquor, and, when unconscious, were taken aboard ship and sold upon arrival in the colonies. In some years as many as ten to fifteen thousand men, women, and children may have been brought to America in this manner.

The indentured's conditions of servitude were far superior to those of the slaves. Generally, the indentured servant was not branded (as the slave often was), he was not forced to perform the field slave's back-breaking labors, his children did not inherit his labor contract, and he was given better food and clothing.[3] If he ran away from his master, his chances of escape were much better than those of the slave. The indentured servant could look forward to eventual freedom and could usually expect a grant of land when his period of service expired. In many cases, he was also promised a sum of money or goods upon termination of service; but he frequently experienced great difficulty in collecting. It has been estimated that only one former indentured servant in ten actually settled upon the land. Some took up trade, and others died in service, returned to Europe, or became demoralized beggars and indigent "poor whites."[4]

The system of apprenticeship as practiced in England and in America was another form of servitude. Under the system, children—generally, the poor and orphans—

would be bound out to a master craftsman in order to learn a trade or craft.[5] The articles of apprenticeship, as harsh and binding as an indenture, were usually for seven years, during which the master craftsman agreed to provide food, clothing, and housing for his apprentice; to educate him in the craft; and to give him a rudimentary education, at least to teach him to read and write. At the end of his apprenticeship the master was also to provide the boy with "freedom dues," usually a small amount of money and a suit of clothing. At the time, it was believed that the system of apprenticeship served to maintain a high standard of craftsmanship. When a boy's apprenticeship of seven years was completed, he usually became a journeyman to or an employee of the master craftsman. Among the craftsmen that most often made use of the system were blacksmiths, shoemakers, carpenters, shipwrights, and tailors.

As suggested earlier, slavery did not gain a stronghold in the New World until the eighteenth century, even though the first black slaves had arrived in the colonies in 1619. Throughout the seventeenth century a large number of slaves lived in the northern colonies, and not merely in the South. In fact, many New England port towns had as great a slave population as Virginia.[6] New York had the largest percentage of slaves in the North, the majority of them working on the large estates in the interior. However, once the plantation economy expanded in the South and slavery became highly profitable, slaves became dominant in the southern colonies. By 1720, for example, South Carolina had more slaves than whites. As early as 1712, slaves accounted for 30 percent of the South's total population.[7] The majority of slaves sent to the North American colonies did not come directly from Africa, but through the markets of the West Indian islands.

By the early eighteenth century, the slave was becoming such a fixture in America that his status was now legally defined. It was proclaimed that he had no legal rights, that he and all his heirs would be in perpetual bondage, that runaways would be severely punished. The planter was expected to feed and clothe him and

Figure 2. *Indentured Servant, 1730.*
This figure, also a runaway, "had on a dark colored broadcloth coat with white metal buttons and long pockets, and a striped ticken jacket and breeches."
Source: From *Pennsylvania Gazette*, No. 99, October 1730. Drawing by author.

173

Figure 3. *Two French West Indies Slaves, 1760s.*
The slaves seen here are wearing only cotton breeches, the
normal working dress for slaves in the West Indies throughout
the eighteenth century.
  Source: From Diderot, *Diderot's Pictorial Encyclopedia
of Trades and Industry.* Drawing by author.

train him to a skill. It was at this time that the skilled
slave drove the unskilled freeman from the South to the
middle colonies. By the end of the century, slavery had
become much less economical, and there was a continual
fear of slave uprisings and insurrections. Nevertheless,
slavery persisted in the South into the nineteenth century
when cotton and sugar production once more increased
its profitability.

DRESS

Slaves, indentured servants, and apprentices, were,
of course, dressed as economically as possible. Again, a
study of the descriptions of runaways offers us an excellent cross-sectional view of the dress of the period. Bonds-
men are seldom described as being dressed in garments
distinctive of a particular occupation (though many
were skilled craftsmen), but most often the runaways
wore everyday working dress. In the southern colonies,
slaves were generally dressed in "negro cloth" or "negro
cotton," a cheap cotton cloth that was white or unbleached and sometimes dyed or striped. Ticking (or
ticken), a cheap linen textile, and oznabrug coarse linen
were much used in clothing indentured servants and
slaves as well as working class people generally.

Figure 4. *Runaway Slave from South Carolina, 1776.*
"Oznabrug shirt, negro cloth breeches, dyed yellow, a red cap
and a pair of boots, one red and the other white."
     Source: From *South Carolina General Gazette,* No. 918,
8 May 1776. Drawing by author.

Figure 5. *South Carolina Slave, 1773.*
This indigo plantation slave wears a simple jacket and trousers
of white or unbleached "negro cloth." The buttons on his jacket
and trousers are probably of lead or wood. Laborers on the
indigo plantations usually went without shoes or hats.
     Source: From a cartouche on a map by Henry Mouzon of
the parish of St. Stephen in Craven County, South Carolina,
1773; William P. Cumming, *The Southeast in Early Maps*
(Chapel Hill, North Carolina, 1958). Drawing by author.

Figure 6. *Runaway Slave Woman from South Carolina, 1776.*
Oznabrug jacket and white woolen petticoats.
  Source: From *South Carolina and American General Gazette,*
27 March 1776. Drawing by author.

Figure 7. *Indentured Servant from New Jersey, 1776.*
"Had on when he went away, a home-spun striped jacket, an
under white thick cloth ditto with pewter buttons, brown
homemade breeches, patched on the knee, an old hat, a black
handkerchief about his neck, coarse black grey stockings."
  Source: From *The Pennsylvania Packet,* 3 June 1776.
Drawing by author.

176

Figure 8. *South Carolina Slave Brought to Camden Gaol, 1777.* "Blue broadcloth coat, German serge breeches, and a rush hat." Rush, or straw, hats were more frequently seen in the southern colonies.

Source: From *South Carolina and American General Gazette,* No. 952, 10 April 1777. Drawing by author.

Figure 9. *South Carolina Slave, 1777.* Checked shirt, cross bar trousers, and small round hat.

Source: From *South Carolina and American General Gazette,* 14 August 1777. Drawing by author.

177

Figure 10. *South Carolina Slaves, 1780-1790.*
The woman wears a white gown and apron; the kerchiefs on her head and around her neck are white with blue stripes. The man wears a black hat with a white band, dark blue jacket with lead buttons, light brown breeches, and light brown waistcoat. The stringed instrument is believed to be a molo, an instrument of the Yoruba people, much resembling a gourd banjo.

Source: From a watercolor by an unknown artist, entitled "The Old Plantation," discovered in Columbia, South Carolina, *Antiques* (February 1975). Drawing by author.

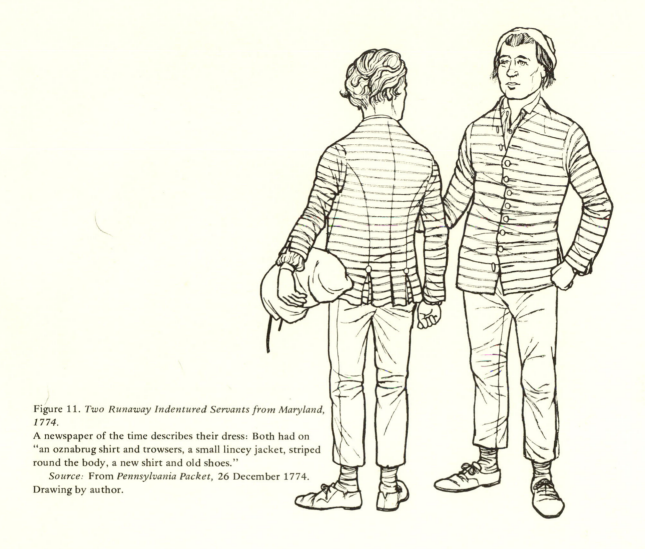

Figure 11. *Two Runaway Indentured Servants from Maryland,
1774.*
A newspaper of the time describes their dress: Both had on
"an oznabrug shirt and trowsers, a small lincey jacket, striped
round the body, a new shirt and old shoes."
    Source: From *Pennsylvania Packet,* 26 December 1774.
Drawing by author.

NOTES

1. Ver Steeg, *The Formative Years, 1607-1763*, pp. 188-189.
2. William P. Randall, *The American Revolution, Mirror of a
    People* (New York, 1973).
3. Ver Steeg, op. cit., p. 191.
4. Randall, op. cit.
5. Ver Steeg, op. cit., p. 196.
6. Ibid., p. 190.
7. Ibid.

(12)
Criminals

As a result of the economic depression that occurred at the end of the French and Indian War, the late middle years of the eighteenth century saw a frightening increase in crime in the colonies. Although the amount of crime never equaled that which existed in the mother country, there were excessive incidents of counterfeiting, theft, burglary, highway robbery, and murder. Some of the violence was committed by seamen, soldiers, laborers, and privateersmen who, left unemployed at the end of the war, turned to professional crime. Another criminal element was the poor of many nations, many of them transported felons, who were now migrating to the cities in large numbers. By Act of Parliament, the authorities in England could now ship "rogues, vagabonds, and sturdy beggars" to the colonies.[1] Once they reached the New World many resumed their old habits.

Counterfeiting was a problem in all the colonies, and shopkeepers of the time had to maintain a constant vigil against it. Murders and burglaries were also widespread in all the colonial cities. Piracy had become a fairly rare offense by mid-century, so much so that the hanging of two men in Newport, Rhode Island, for piracy in 1760 attracted a crowd of five or six thousand spectators.[2] Such crimes as highway robbery and burglary continued, though they were more frequent during the various colonial wars, when large numbers of soldiers and sailors were quartered in colonial towns.[3]

By mid-century, too, prostitution had become a serious problem in the cities, having flourished during the colonial wars. The prostitutes of the maritime ports were especially well patronized. It has been shown that, in 1744, the "battery" in New York was a good place to find a woman, for "the place was the general rendezvous of the fair sex of that profession after sunset." All of the colonial cities had houses of prostitution.[4]

As was true of the other major cities, Philadelphia experienced many kinds of crime during the 1750s, particularly homicide, rape, assault, and petty larceny. It is interesting to note that the cruel punishments of the day—hanging, flogging, and mutilation—did little

Figure 1. *English Highwayman, 1750.*
Here the notorious highwayman known as the "Golden Farmer"
is shown robbing a poor tinker on the road.
   Source: A print in the author's collection, by J. Nichols,
1750.

to discourage the commission of crime. A Philadelphian observed in February 1758 that, "Thefts and petty robberies are now become so common in and about the city that no less than eight persons were last Saturday chastised at a cart's tail in the Marketplace, and carted about and whipt at the Public Corners of the Town, notwithstanding the rigidness of the season."[5] Punishments varied somewhat from colony to colony. In some areas convicted felons were for some crimes "nayled by both ears to the Pillory, 3 nails in each eare, and the nailes to be slit out."[6]

The severity of punishment can perhaps be better understood today if one remembers that it was an eighteenth-century belief that the criminal deliberately chose a life of crime and that his wickedness had to be punished. Publicly inflicted punishment was thought to have a good effect on the population generally and to act as a deterrent to those so tempted. There was no thought given to rehabilitating or reforming the criminal.[7]

New York was infested by "rogues and thieves aplenty" after 1749, and by 1753 the town was a center for organized vice. It is recorded that in 1755 one Thomas Pearson, a mate aboard the HMS *Mercury*,

Figure 2. *English Armed Thief, Circa 1808.*
The thief wears a short tattered jacket and trousers. A veil
covers his face.
   Source: An unidentified print in the author's collection.

killed a prostitute whom he claimed had picked his
pocket while plying her trade. This type of crime had
become a rather common occurrence in colonial seaports.

Thieves (as well as paupers) were sold at public auction
in the colonies during the eighteenth century.[8] The sale
of poor people, it is recorded, was a particularly pathetic
spectacle. The auction normally took place in a tavern
where a sad little group of homeless creatures, usually
elderly folk and young children, would be sold to the
highest bidder. Such children were known as "bound
boys" and "bound girls."[9]

DRESS

Highwaymen were often elaborately dressed in the
best upper class fashion of the day. Others affected the
dress of the professions. For example, in a description
of three American highwaymen who attacked a mail
wagon in 1818, the attackers were reported to be dressed
"in sailor's trowsers and round jackets. . . two wearing
hats and the other wearing a silk handkerchief tied
around his head."

Figure 3. *Two German Prisoners, 1770.*
Both are in irons and they are accompanied by a guard in horseman's cap and boots.
Source: A print in the author's collection, by Daniel Chodowieckis, 1770.

Figure 4. *American Horse Thief, Circa 1776.*
"Light coloured surtout coat with black horn buttons, his under coat a mixed colour, inclining on the red, a black velvet waistcoat, the hind parts black callimancoe, a pair of buckskin breeches, something sullied, plated buckles, ruffled shirt, white neckcloth, dark coloured hair, mixed with grey, and club'd up with a false tail."
Source: From a newspaper advertisement appearing in New Jersey during the Revolution. Drawing by author.

Figure 5. *Horse Thief from South Carolina, 1777.*
Russian drab breeches, white shirt, and striped blue and white upper and under jackets.
Source: From *South Carolina and American General Gazette*, No. 970, 7 August 1777. Drawing by author.

Figure 6. *English Seaman and Prostitute, 1785.*
"A Rich Privateer Brought Safely to Port" is the sardonic
caption of the print from which this drawing is derived. An
English seaman of about 1785 is shown about to be taken in
by a well-dressed prostitute.

   Source: From a watercolor by Robert Dighton, circa 1785,
in George, *Hogarth to Cruikshank*, p. 66. Drawing by author.

Figure 7. *English Prostitute, 1780.*
Dark blue gown, white apron, grey gloves, and blue and yellow
ribbons in her hat.

   Source: From a print in the author's collection, by Robert
Sayer, London. Drawing by author.

NOTES

1. Barck and Leffler, *Colonial America.*
2. Ibid.
3. Ibid.
4. Bridenbaugh, *Cities in Revolt.*
5. Barck and Leffler, op. cit.
6. Ibid.
7. Ibid.
8. Ibid.
9. Earle, *Stage-Coach and Tavern Days.*

(13)
National
Groupings

Beginning in the latter part of the seventeenth century and accelerating in the eighteenth, new nationalities and numerous religious sects, including the Quakers, Moravians, and Pietists, migrated to the New World in massive numbers. Among the non-English were the Germans, Scotch-Irish, Irish, Scots, Swedes, French Huguenots, and Welsh. Most of the new migrants came to the English rather than the French or Spanish colonies, primarily because they had heard reports that land was cheaper there and, perhaps more important, that the English settlements would offer a haven from religious persecution.[1] Significantly, the majority of these new settlers were from the lower classes, thus bolstering the labor force at a time when cheap labor was in great demand.

With New England's reputation for narrow religious views, understandably few of these national groupings headed there. Rather, the South and the middle colonies received the overwhelming share. For example, by 1770 nearly 250,000 Germans had migrated to America; approximately 70 percent of this figure came to New York, Pennsylvania, and New Jersey, with Pennsylvania alone getting 50 percent of the total. In contrast, fewer than 1 percent went to New England.[2] Like the Germans the Scotch-Irish, Irish, and Scots also were attracted to the middle and southern colonies.

The Scotch-Irish, highland Scots, and lowland Scots made up a good part of the migratory wave of colonists who later pushed through the mountains inland to the West. The highland Scots, a smaller group than the Scotch-Irish, began migrating to America in substantial numbers around 1729. Most came to North Carolina where they soon formed a considerable settlement in the upper Cape Fear Valley. More flocked to the colonies after the rebellion of 1745 failed, at the end of which the English brutally set about dismantling the clan system of the highlands. After the great defeat at Culloden, the rebellious clansmen were offered a pardon by the king if they would agree to emigrate to America. They accepted the offer with enthusiasm. For years afterward, one of the highlanders' favorite songs was "Going to

Figure 1. *George Dillwyn, Pennsylvania Quaker, 1738-1820.*
Simple unadorned suit of clothes and round hat.
   Source: From Amelia Mott Gummere, *The Quaker, A Study in Costume* (New York, 1901). Drawing by author.

Seek a Fortune in North Carolina." This migration, composed after 1746 of transported prisoners and pardoned rebels, continued during and after the American Revolution.

Not only did the non-English migrants add immensely to the total population, but they also introduced new ideas and customs and began to shape a new style of working class. Members of this class, particularly the urban workers, became the most stalwart defenders of the rebel cause throughout the long struggle for independence.

DRESS

Quakers

With minor variations, the dress of the Quakers resembled that of various other religious sects. Most of the fundamentalist sects, including the Quakers, Amish, Dunkards, and Pietists, advocated plainness and simplicity in dress; thus, the details of their attire always conformed with these ideals. Because of this similarity, the Quaker dress will be described here as representative.

Contrary to popular beliefs, Quaker garb did not differ in cut or style from that worn in England at the time they set sail for the New World. Rather, the distinction of the Quaker's dress lay in its elimination of all decoration or any hint of luxury in his attire. Hence, braid, plumes, and laces were generally absent.[3] This restriction on ornateness did not extend to the quality of materials permitted. In fact, the Quaker's garments were far from cheap and were often as fine as those of the upper classes.

The men wore coats, with broad skirts to the knee, collarless waistcoats, cocked and broad-brimmed hats, and shoe roses. Some wore wigs—though less spectacular ones than those in fashion—and others wore their own hair, usually long.[4] In the early years, the women wore full skirts gathered into pleats, green aprons over their gowns, elbow-length sleeves, long-eared or round-eared caps, and hoods variously known as cardinals, capuchins, or riding hoods.[5] Later, the green aprons gave way to gayer, more fashionable colors, and the riding hoods and caps, to the skimming-dish hats of the modern

188

Quaker bonnets—large white beaver hats with a low crown, tied with ribbons under the chin.

The more orthodox Quakers did not conform to changing styles of dress. However, many who lived in more fashionable circles yielded to the new modes. A Quaker from New Jersey deplored such transgressions and feared the consequences: "The young men wearing their hats set up behind and next its likely will be a ribbon to tie their hair up behind. And the girls in Pennsylvania have their necks set off with a black ribbon— a sorrowful sight indeed."[6]

Figure 2. *Four Varieties of Quaker Hats, Late Eighteenth Century.* None of the hats is cocked up. On two of the hats the looping has been slackened, thus lowering the brim.
Source: From Gummere, op. cit. Drawing by author.

The Dutch

By mid-century, New York City was becoming a truly cosmopolitan port, and the Dutch language and customs had already fallen out of use. In rural New York State, however, the patroon system of landholding was still employed until the Revolution. In addition, the Dutch language was spoken in several counties. As for dress, we have Dr. Alexander Hamilton's description in 1744: "Women [in Albany] in general, both old and young are the hardest favoured ever I beheld. Their old women wear a conical head dress, large pendants, short petticoats."[7]

Germans

By the eighteenth century, the general appearance of German working people was not too different from the English. However, German peasant costume from rural areas was distinctly at variance with the typical American dress.

Welsh

The dress of Welsh women was more distinctive than that of the men. While the men wore the usual working class garments—coats or jackets, breeches, and waist-coats—women in Wales dressed in coarse, sky blue linens and worsted stockings of the same color. As was true of lower class people in England, especially in rural areas, both sexes wore many of the same items of clothing: both wore round felt hats, shoes with buckles, and,

189

Figure 3. *Quaker, 1787.*
Large round hat and simple suit devoid of frills and lace.
   Source: From Grassett de St. Sauveur, *Costumes Civils Actuels de Tous les Peuples Connus* (Paris, 1787). Drawing by author.

sometimes, coats, cloaks, and jackets. The Welsh country woman's dress reached its final form in the eighteenth century. It was in fact much the same as the dress worn by English country women, except for the kind of material used: Welsh cloth was mainly wool.

The French

The French, who did not migrate to their native colonies settled primarily in colonial Maine (then part of Massachusetts) and South Carolina, near Charleston. The dress of French working people was similar to that of the English.

Scotch-Irish and Scots

The dress of the lowland Scots, the Scotch-Irish, and the Irish was similar to that of other working people in Britain. The highland Scots, however, did have a distinctive dress—that of highland tartans with checked patterns and bonnets—and they clung to it for some time after their arrival in America. The Loyalists at the battle of Moore's Creek in 1775, for instance, are recorded as wearing highland dress and being accompanied by pipers.

Figure 4. *Dutch Woman, North Netherlands, Circa 1700.*
Her hair is cropped short, and she wears a narrow apron.
  Source: From Oakes and Hill, *Rural Costume.* Drawing
by author.

Figure 5. *Dutch Merchant, 1762.*
The hat, short jacket, and full breeches resemble those of the
rural Dutch countryman of the eighteenth century.
  Source: From "The Times," by William Hogarth, Plate 1,
1762; also Oakes and Hill, op. cit. Drawing by author.

Figure 6. *German Woman, Late Eighteenth Century*.
The dress shown here was typical for the area around Ulm.
Source: From Oakes and Hill, op. cit. Drawing by author.

192

Figure 7. *Welsh Country Woman, Late Eighteenth Century.*
The felt hat shown here was worn by women in Britain over a
hundred years before. Her open-fronted skirt is fastened back
to show her striped petticoat. She wears a long apron to protect
the petticoat front. A small checked shawl covers the low neck-
line of her gown, which is of striped Welsh wool.

   Source: From a painting by J. C. Ibbetson, "Street Scene
in Llangollen," Denbighshire; also F. G. Payne, *Welsh Peasant
Costume* (Cardiff, Wales, 1964). Drawing by author.

Figure 8. *French Housewife, Mid-eighteenth Century.*
Her gown, apron, and linen cap are in no way distinctive, being
similar to the dress of any colonial American or English housewife of the time.

   Source: From a print in the author's collection, marked
"La Marque, Paris, 1765."

Figure 9. *Lowland Scottish Man and Woman Conversing with Lawyer, 1802.*
The man on the left wears a Scots bonnet, great coat, and gaiters. The woman wears a hood, spotted shawl, and checked apron.

   Source: A print in the author's collection, by John Kay, 1802.

194

John Steel of the Parish of Little Dunkeld Perthshire Aged 109 drawn from the Life

Figure 10. *Man from Little Dunkeld, Perthshire, 1808.*
Battered cocked hat with the loopings barely visible and a cord
around the crown.
    Source: A print in the author's collection, by John Kay,
1808.

Figure 11. *Working Class Scottish Woman, 1792.*
She wears a short workman's jacket. Her apron is bunched up around her waist, and she carries her load by means of a head band.

    Source: A print in the author's collection, by John Kay, 1792.

Figure 12. *Scots Piper, 1790.*
Highland bonnet, great coat, and waistcoat bound with leather belt.

Source: A print in the author's collection, by John Kay, 1790.

NOTES

1. Ver Steeg, *The Formative Years,* p. 166.
2. Ibid., p. 167
3. Warwick, Pitz, and Wyckoff, *Early American Dress,* p. 201.
4. Ibid., p. 203.
5. Earle, *Two Centuries of Costume in America,* p. 603.
6. Amelia M. Gummere, *The Quaker, A Study in Costume* (London, 1901).
7. *A Gentleman's Progress: The Itinerarium of Dr. Alexander Hamilton.*

Glossary

Apron. Generally of coarse linen, canvas, or baize and worn by workingmen and women. Leather aprons were called "barvells" (see *Barvell* below).

Baize (also *Baise, Bayes*). A cheap, coarse, woolen cloth which was made in many colors and was used for trousers, aprons, jackets, and gowns.

Band. A linen collar stiffened with starch; worn by clergymen and members of the legal profession.

Banyan (also *Banian, Banjan*). A loose gown adopted for wear by the British in India; worn principally by upper and middle class people of both sexes when at home. Elegant banyans of costly materials were sometimes worn as street dress.

Barvell. A leather apron; worn principally by smiths, woodworkers, and fishermen.

Batts. Low, sturdy shoes, laced in front rather than buckled.

Bearskin. A rough, sturdy material; used for workmen's coats and jackets.

Bob Wig. A short, close-fitting wig; worn by boys and men of all classes, 1725 through 1775-1780.

Bodice. The upper part of a woman's dress; laced either in front or in back, or in both front and back.

Bonnet. A small head covering worn by men and women, usually without a brim. Quilted bonnets and "Kitty Fisher bonnets" were worn by colonial women in the 1720s and thereafter. Blue woolen bonnets were the headgear of the Scots Highland men.

Boots. Fishermen wore leather boots which looked much like rubber seaman's boots of today. Postillions wore heavy leather boots known as postillions' boots. Cavalry men wore leather dragoon boots.

Breeches. Buttoned at the waist and knee, and buckled (sometimes tied) at the knee below the buttons, breeches were made from all kinds of materials throughout the eighteenth century. Workmen's breeches were usually made from oznabrug linen, leather, ticking, shag, and, sometimes in New England, from deerskin and mooseskin.

Broadcloth. A fine woolen cloth; worn chiefly by the upper classes.

Brogues. Coarse, stout shoes made of rawhide; worn by working men, especially in Scotland and Ireland.

Brooch. A clasp of iron, brass, gold, or silver used for fastening clothing; worn especially by Scots Highland people to fasten their plaids.

Calash (also *Calèche*). A hood made to pull over a woman's head. It was introduced into England from France in about 1765.

Calico. A cotton fabric originally imported from India, and worn by all classes. The name was finally given to any cotton fabric.

Callimanco. A glazed, worsted fabric made in striped, checked, or plain pattern; worn by all classes.

Cambric. A fine linen.

Camlet (also *Camblet*). A plain or twilled cloth, sometimes of wool, silk, or other mixtures; used in making jackets, cloaks, and coats.

Canvas. A coarse, woven cloth of hemp or flax; used for making workmen's trousers, aprons, and jackets.

Cap. A small, close-fitting head covering; worn by working class men and women. Seamen wore knitted "Monmouth caps" and working women often wore linen "mob caps."

Cape. The turned-down collar on a coat or jacket.

Capote. A hooded blanket coat with tie fastenings in the front; worn by farmers, soldiers, and frontiersmen.

Capuchin (also *Capuchon*). A hooded cloak worn by women in the fashion of the garment worn by the Capuchin monks. This cloak, also known as a Riding Hood, was fashionable in the first half of the eighteenth century.

Cardinal. A hooded cloak, usually of scarlet cloth; worn by women during the first half of the eighteenth century.

Cassock. A clergyman's garment made of black cloth, reaching to the ankles and buttoning down the front with tight, long sleeves.

Castor. Originally, a beaver felt from which hats were made; later, a cheaper felt hat, made from a felt mixed with wool.

Chemise. A woman's undergarment, knee length, with

200

short sleeves; made of linen, homespun, or cotton.

Cherridary. A cotton stuff resembling gingham; imported from India after 1712.

Cloak. A loose outergarment, often made of camlet, with a lining of a different color; worn by both sexes.

Clock. Embroidery at the ankle of expensive stockings; worn by the upper classes.

Clogs. Overshoes made of canvas or leather, with wooden soles, to raise the wearer above the dirt or mud, in a similar manner to pattens; worn primarily in rural areas.

Clout. A kerchief of coarse linen, worn knotted about the head.

Coatee. A short coat of military style, reaching halfway down the thigh.

Cockade. A bit of ribbon in the shape of a bow, tucked behind a loop attached to a button on the left side of a cocked hat. Cockades were worn by soldiers and state officials and by those affecting a patriotic appearance. They were also worn in the hats of servants attached to military or naval officers or state officials.

Country Boots. Strips of blanket cloth secured around the leg, at the knee, and the ankle; worn by lower class people in lieu of leather boots or leggings.

Crocus. A coarse stuff made up into clothing for poor people and slaves.

Deerskin. New England farmers and soldiers wore breeches of dressed deerskin and mooseskin.

Dimity. A cotton fabric with fine ribs, originally from India; worn by all classes.

Dornex. A heavy, coarse linen resembling canvas; used for making workingmen's smocks and trousers.

Dowlas. A heavy, coarse linen used for making shirts and smocks for working class people.

Dreadnaught. See *Fearnaught.*

Drugget. A woolen fabric used mainly for making coats and jackets; worn by working people.

Duck. A strong, white linen fabric without a twill, used for making belts and straps where leather was not available and workmen's jackets and trousers.

201

Duffels. A coarse, woolen stuff used in making coats and jackets.

Durant. A strong, glazed woolen stuff, sometimes called "everlasting."

Dutch Bonnet. A straw bonnet worn by women, turned up in front and back.

Embroidery. Fancy needlework used for the decoration of dress. Gentlemen's and military officers' coats often had ornately embroidered buttonholes in the 1750s.

Facings. The lapels, cuffs, and color of a soldier's coat, done in contrasting colors to the coat itself.

Fearnaught (also *Dreadnaught*). A thick cloth with a long pile used for making heavy surtout coats and thick winter jackets.

Felt. Material used in making hats. Felt is not woven but formed by matting together by moisture and heat under pressure. Beaver felt was used to make hats, but there were cheaper felts, such as castor, usually worn by working men.

Ferret. A narrow ribbon or tape of cotton or silk; used mainly for binding, such as buttonholes.

Frieze. A coarse, heavy woolen cloth; often used in making workmen's coats.

Fustian. A coarse, cheap textile of mixed linen and cotton; used for making coats, jackets, and trousers.

Garters. Bands used to hold up the stocking. Secured by a small buckle, the garter fit under the knee band of a man's breeches.

Golosh. A wooden-soled shoe secured by means of straps over the instep. worn over the ordinary shoe in bad weather.

Grogram. A coarse taffeta, of silk and wool, woven diagonally; used in the American colonies.

Haling Hands. Mittens, made of wool or felt, the palms of which were often reinforced with leather; worn by working people, particularly seamen and fishermen.

Hat. Beaver and castor hats were largely imported from England. Both working men and women wore hats of cheap castor, sometimes of straw or canvas,

202

usually uncocked or round. Hats were cocked up
in a variety of fashions, none of which was particularly
sensible for working people. The hat could be simply
cocked up behind or on one side, but most often
was cocked up and secured with loops on three sides.
Some seafaring men wore knitted hats with a brim
all around.

Hunting Shirt. A smock-like outershirt usually made of
coarse linen; worn by hunters and soldiers. See also
Rifle Shirt.

Jacket. Outer and underjackets were worn by all types
of working men throughout the eighteenth century.
Early in the century they reached almost to the
knee; as the century wore on they became shorter
until, by 1800, they came to the hip. Workmen's
jackets were single- and double-breasted.

Jean. A cotton cloth used for men's summer clothing.
It became very popular in the United States at the
turn of the nineteenth century.

Jockey Cap. A cap with a peaked front and round crown,
usually decorated with a ribbon around the crown.
It was shaped much like the jockey cap of today.

Jumps. A loose bodice worn by women. Also a short,
loose jacket ("jump jack coat") reaching to the
thighs and worn by men.

Kersey. A coarse, woolen cloth originally from Yorkshire.
It was used for stockings before the introduction of
knitting.

Kirtle. A woman's body garment with sleeves, reaching
to the floor and worn under the gown. Also a kind
of short jacket without skirts.

Lappet. Pendants descending from the sides of a woman's
indoor cap, cometimes tied below the chin.

Lawn. A fine, semi-transparent linen cloth, similar to
cambric.

Leggings. In colonial America, a buckskin or cloth
Indian leg covering which extended from the ankle
almost to the crotch and was fastened to a waistbelt
by strings. The white settlers adopted them in a
variety of styles.

Monmouth Cap. A seafarer's knitted cap closely re-

sembling the knitted watch cap worn by seamen
today.

Nankeen. A yellow cotton cloth imported from China,
often made into waistcoats and breeches.

Neck Cloth. Worn by both sexes throughout the colonies.
Neck cloths worn by working people were generally
simple kerchiefs knotted about the neck.

Oznabrug (variously spelled). A cheap and coarse but
strong linen made originally in Oznabrug, Germany;
worn by both sexes in the lower classes.

Pattens. A platform overshoe with a wooden sole into
which iron rings were set to raise the shoe above
mud or water. It was fastened to the foot by leather
straps.

Petticoat. A woman's garment worn by all classes and
made in a great variety of materials. Quilted petticoats were very popular in the mid- to late eighteenth
century.

Petticoat Trousers (also "Slops"). Short, wide trousers
reaching to the knee, made of coarse linen or old
sail canvas. They were worn by seamen as a
working overgarment to protect the breeches
worn beneath.

Pig Tail Wig. Wig with a braided tail tied with a ribbon.
It was very popular among middle-class men in the
mid-eighteenth century.

Pinner. A woman's indoor headress made of fine lace
or linen. It was close-fitting and had long tabs or
lappets that hung down the sides.

Pockets. In addition to its conventional meaning, pockets
in the eighteenth century referred to a small pouch
or bag, not part of a garment, fastened by a string
to the waist.

Polonese. A woman's long-sleeved garment resembling
a coat, opening down the front and with a hood at
the back. The word is a corruption of "Polonaise"
or "Polish."

Pug. A short cape, usually made of cloth, with a hood
attached; worn by women.

Pump. A light, long quartered shoe with a thin sole;
worn by seamen as part of their shoregoing finery.

204

Queue. The tail of a wig.

Ramall. A shawl or neckerchief worn over a woman's shoulders.

Ratteen. A thick, twilled woolen cloth.

Rifle Shirt. A smock-type outer shirt worn by riflemen. It was often decorated with fringes and made of linen or cloth.

Robings. The decorative part of a woman's gown, such as lapels, roughly corresponding to the facings on a soldier's coat.

Roquelaure (also *Roquelo* or *Rocket*). A heavy cloak made with two small capes and usually done in bright blue or red; worn by both sexes.

Ruffles. Made of fine cambric linen or lawn. Ruffles were attached to the cuff of the sleeve and at the throat of a gentleman's body shirt.

Sagathy. A woolen stuff resembling serge.

Serge. A woolen or silk twilled fabric. It sometimes combined both wool and silk.

Shag. A worsted cloth, rather shaggy in appearance, which was frequently used for making linings.

Shalloon. A woolen fabric used for lining clothes.

Sherry Vallies. A long legging buttoning up the side and worn over a man's breeches to protect a horseman from mud and rain.

Shift. An undershirt or chemise made of linen. It was the standard woman's undergarment during the colonial period.

Shoepack. A moccasin-like shoe made of tanned leather without an outer sole; worn in rural areas.

Skilts. Short, wide trousers, coming just below the knee; much the same as the sailor's petticoat trousers; worn by country people.

Sleeves. Separate, protective sleeves tied to the arm with cords or ribbons; much worn by butchers to protect their shirt sleeves when working.

Slops (also *Slop-hose*). Wide-kneed breeches worn by seamen. Also, another name for petticoat trousers.

Slyders. Overalls; worn by rural people.

Smock. An outer shirt made of coarse linen or cloth, often reaching below the knees; worn by farmers,

205

herders, and waggoners. It was quite similar to the
rifle shirt or hunting shirt of the Continental soldier.

Snow Shoe (called "Rackets" in the eighteenth century).
An Indian invention adopted by the whites which
was used by New England country people and frontier
militia in the northern colonies.

Spatterdash. Short leggings of canvas, cloth, or leather,
buttoned down the side and coming down from the
mid-calf to cover the buckle on the shoe; much worn
by country people and soldiers.

Steinkirk. A man's cravat, folded carelessly, with the
ends usually tucked through the top buttonholes
of the coat; fashionable in the first half of the
eighteenth century.

Stock. A neck cloth, successor to the cravat, which
was buckled at the back of the neck with a narrow
buckle known as a stock buckle.

Surtout. A large overcoat, usually single-breasted, with
one or more spreading capes; also known as a "wrap
rascal."

Swanskin. A fleece-like cloth similar to light flannel;
used in making waistcoats and lining clothing.

Tabby. A watered silk.

Tartan. The plaid cloth woven and worn by the people

of the Scottish highlands in the first half of the
eighteenth century.

Tongs. Overalls of coarse linen or cotton.

Trews. Close-bodied trousers made of tartan cloth; worn
by upper class Scottish highland men.

Trousers. A garment extending from waist to ankles, much
like modern trousers in cut; made in a variety of different materials; worn by working people and seafarers.

Turban. A colored scarf fastened about the base of the
crown of a dragoon's cap or helmet, knotted at the
back and often terminating with fringed tassels.

Waistcoat. A waist-length underjacket worn by men
throughout the eighteenth century. In the early
part of the century, waistcoats were worn with
skirts extending almost to the knees. The skirts of
the waistcoat became shorter later in the century.
By 1800 skirts were removed altogether, and the
waistcoat became straight-bottomed. Made with and
without sleeves. Synonymous with vest.

Wig. Worn by men of all classes until about 1780-1790
when they gradually fell out of fashion. Wigs were
made in a great variety of styles and colors.

Worsted. A woolen cloth originally made in Worstead,
England.

Bibliography

Album of American History. New York, 1944.

Alden, John R. *The South in the Revolution, 1763-1789.* (Baton Rouge, 1957).

American Heritage Book of the Revolution. New York, 1958.

American Heritage History of Colonial America. New York, 1967.

American Heritage Magazine. Vols. I-XXIII. New York,

The American Neptune, Maritime Quarterly. Salem, Massachusetts, 1920-1949.

American Printmaking, the First 150 Years. Smithsonian Institution Press, Washington, D.C., 1969.

Armes, Ethel. *Nancy Shippen, Her Journal Book.* New York, 1935.

Barck, Oscar T., and Lefler, Hugh T. *Colonial America.* New York, 1958.

Bartolozzi, F. *The Months.* London, 1788.

Bayne-Powell, Rosamond. *Travelers in 18th Century England.* London, 1951.

Belknap, Waldran P., Jr. *American Colonial Painting.* Cambridge, Massachusetts, 1959.

Bernardo Bellotto. Dresden, 1963.

Bonanni, Filippo. *The Showcase of Musical Instruments.* New York, 1964.

The Book of Trades. London, 1808.

Boorstin, Daniel J. *The Americans, the Colonial Experience.* New York, 1958.

Bradfield, Nancy. *Costume in Detail, 1730-1930.* London, 1968.

Bridenbaugh, Carl. *Cities in Revolt: Urban Life in America, 1743-1776.* New York, 1955.

Brookner, Anita. *Watteau.* Middlesex, 1967.

Catchpenny Prints, by Bowles and Carver. London, 1970.

Chodowieckis, Daniel. *Künstlerfahrt nach Danzig im Jahre 1773.* Berlin, 1908.

Cirker, B., ed. *1800 Woodcuts by Thos. Bewick and His School.* New York, 1962.

Cobban, Aldred, ed. *The 18th Century.* New York, 1969.

Copeland, Peter. *Everyday Dress of the American Revolution.* New York, 1974.

Cunnington, Phillis, and Beard, Charles. *Dictionary of English Costume.* London, 1960.

Cunnington, C. Willet, Lucas, Catherine, and Mansfield, Alan. *Occupational Costume in England from the Eleventh Century to 1914.* London, 1967.

Davenport, Milia. *The Book of Costume.* Vol. 2. New York, 1948.

Decker, Malcolm. *Brink of Revolution.* New York, 1964.

Diderot, Denis. *Diderot's Pictorial Encyclopedia of Trades and Industry.* 2 vols. New York, 1959. (Dover reprint.)

Dunbar, J. Telfer. *Highland Dress.* London, 1962.

Earle, Alice Morse. *Costume of Colonial Times.* New York, 1894.

_____. *Stage-Coach and Tavern Days*. New York, 1969. (Dover reprint.)

_____. *Two Centuries of Costume in America*. 2 vols. New York, 1903. (Reprinted 1970.)

Fearon, Henry B. *Sketches of America*. New York, 1818.

Fitzpatrick, John. *The Writings of George Washington*. Washington, D.C., 1931.

Gaunt, William. *The Great Century of British Painting— Hogarth to Turner*. London, 1971.

A Gentleman's Progress: The Itinerarium of Dr. Alexander Hamilton, 1744. Chapel Hill, North Carolina, 1948.

George, M. Dorothy. *Hogarth to Cruikshank, Social Change in Graphic Satire*. New York, 1967.

Glen, James, and Johnston, George M. *Colonial South Carolina*. Columbia, South Carolina, 1951.

Gorsline, Douglas. *What People Wore*. New York, 1952.

Gosse, Philip. *History of Piracy*. New York, 1946.

Gummere, Amelia M. *The Quaker, A Study in Costume*. London, 1901.

Hazlett, W. Carew. *The Livery Companies of the City of London*. London, 1892.

Heal, Ambrose. *London Tradesmen's Cards of the Eighteenth Century*. New York, 1968.

Hesketh, Christian. *Tartans*. New York, 1972.

The Illustrated History of Paris and the Parisians. New York, 1958.

Jackson, Melvin H., and De Beer, Charles. *Eighteenth Century Gunfoundery*. Washington, D.C., 1974.

Jarrett, Dudley. *British Naval Dress*. London, 1960.

John Singleton Copeley. National Gallery of Art and Smithsonian Institution, Washington, D.C., 1965.

Kapp, Friedrich. *Life of Steuben*. New York, 1859.

Klinger, Robert L. *Distaff Sketch Book*. Union City, Tennessee, 1974.

_____. *Sketchbook '76*. Washington, D.C., 1967.

Kohler, Carl. *A History of Costume*. New York, 1963.

Kybalova, L., Herbenova, O., and Lamarova, M. *The Pictorial Encyclopedia of Fashion*. New York, 1968.

Lamb, Roger. *Occurrences During the Late American War*. Dublin, 1809.

Lawson, Cecil C. P. *History of the Uniforms of the British Army*. London, 1940-1966.

Lefferts, Charles M. *Uniforms of the War of the American Revolution*. New York, 1926.

Lemisch, Jesse. "Jack Tar in the Streets: Merchant Seamen in the Politics of Revolutionary America," *William and Mary Quarterly* 25 (July 1968).

Les Combattants Français de la Guerre Americaine, 1778-1783. Paris, 1903.

Macphersen Collection of Naval Prints and Paintings. Green-
    wich, England.
Manuscript Collections and Microfilm Collections of Early
    American Newspapers, Library of Congress, Washington,
    D.C.
Manuscript Collections of the National Archives, Washington,
    D.C.
Manuscript Collections of the Virginia State Library, Richmond,
    Virginia.
The Mariner's Mirror. London, 1921-1945.
McClellan, Elizabeth. *History of American Costume.* New York,
    1904. (Reprinted 1969.)
Mercer, Henry. *Ancient Carpenters Tools.* Doylstown, Penn-
    sylvania, 1960.
New York in the Revolution. Albany, New York, 1904.
Oakes, Alma, and Hill, Margot H. *Rural Costume.* London,
    1970.
Oppé, A. P. *The Drawings of Paul and Thomas Sandby in the
    Collection of His Majesty the King at Windsor Castle.*
    Oxford, 1947.
Painting in England, 1700-1850. Virginia Museum of Fine
    Arts. 1963.
Paintings and Drawings at Wilton House. London, 1968.
Paston, George. *Social Caricature in the 18th Century.*
    London, 1905.
Pennsylvania in the War of the Revolution. Harrisburg,
    Pennsylvania, 1895.
Pyne, William Henry. *Etchings of Rustic Figures.* London, 1814.
_____. *Microcosm.* London, 1806.
Raines, Robert. *Marcellus Laroon.* New York and London,
    1966.
Rankin, Hugh. *The North Carolina Continentals.* Chapel Hill,
    North Carolina, 1971.
Robinson, Charles N. *The British Tar in Fact and Fiction.*
    London, 1909.
Salaman, Malcolm, C. *Old English Mezzotints.* London, 1910.
Sellers, Charles C. *Portraits and Miniatures by Charles Wilson
    Peale.* Philadelphia, 1952.
Sherrill, Charles H. *French Memories of 18th Century America.*
    New York, 1915.
Shesgreen, Sean. *Engravings by Hogarth.* New York, 1973.
Singleton, Esther. *Social New York Under the Georges, 1714-
    1776.* New York, 1902.
Stryker, William S. *Documents Relating to the Revolutionary
    History of the State of New Jersey.* Trenton, New Jersey,
    1901.
Travels in America, by Moreau de Saint Méry, 1792-93. New
    York, 1953.
Travels of William Bartram. Philadelphia, 1791.

Van St. Clara, Abraham. *Iets Voor Allen, Zynde een Verhandeling en Verbeelding Van allerhande, Standen, Studien, Konsten, Wetenschappen, Handwerken,* Abraham Van St. Clara. (Amsterdam, 1719).

Warwick, Edward, Pitz, Henry, and Wyckoff, Alexander. *Early American Dress: The Colonial and Revolutionary Periods.* New York, 1965.

The Watercolor Drawings of Thomas Rowlandson. New York, 1947.

Waterhouse, Ellis. *Gainsborough.* London, 1958.

Webster, Mary. *Francis Wheatly.* London, 1970.

Welsh Peasant Costume. Cardiff, 1964.

The Whale. New York, 1968.

Wharton, Anne H. *Social Life in the Early Republic.* New York, 1902.

Wilhelm, Jacques. *Histoire de la Mode.* Paris, 1955.

Willett, C., and Cunnington, Phillis. *Handbook of English Costume in the 18th Century.* London, 1964.

Wilson, Everett B. *Early America at Work.* New York, 1963.

Yankee Doodle Boy, Joseph Plumb Martin. New York, 1964.

Index

214

217

About the Author

Peter F. Copeland was formerly chief historical illustrator for the Smithsonian Institution. He is currently involved in an undersea project in the Carribbean. His academic specialty is the United States Revolution and military and civilian dress of the eighteenth century.

Recent Titles in
CONTRIBUTIONS IN AMERICAN HISTORY
Series Editor: *Jon L. Wakelyn*

Confederate Women
Bell Irvin Wiley

Battles Lost and Won: Essays from Civil War History
John T. Hubbell, Editor

Beyond the Civil War Synthesis: Political Essays of the
    Civil War Era
Robert P. Swierenga, Editor

Roosevelt and Romanism: Catholics and American
    Diplomacy, 1937-1945
George Q. Flynn

Roots of Tragedy: The United States and the Struggle
    for Asia, 1945-1953
Lisle A. Rose

Henry A. Wallace and American Foreign Policy
J. Samuel Walker

Retreat from Reform: The Prohibition Movement in
    the United States, 1890-1913
Jack S. Blocker, Jr.

A New Birth of Freedom: The Republican Party and
    Freedmen's Rights, 1861-1866
Herman Belz

When Farmers Voted Red: The Gospel of Socialism in
    the Oklahoma Countryside, 1910-1924
Garin Burbank

Essays in Nineteenth-Century American Legal History
Wythe Holt, Editor

Henry Highland Garnet: A Voice of Black Radicalism
    in the Nineteenth Century
Joel Schor

The Prophet's Army: Trotskyists in America, 1928-1941
Constance Ashton Myers

American Revolutionary: A Biography of General
    Alexander McDougall
William L. MacDougall